CW01338019

Going Alone

—

*Creating a life of purpose in a
universe without apparent meaning*

By Kurt Bell
Art by Emily Bell

For David Bixler
Who showed us the wild...

Reviews of Going Alone

"Interesting is an insufficient and effeminate word to describe such depth, darkness, and hope you seem to aim to provide. Deep is better suited to describe the first twenty or so pages I've read thus far... Death is another word I would associate with it, too. Truly, it's a little death this book of yours. Because when I read, I don't just read, I adopt, integrate and discard. A book is powerful that causes you to kill a part of you and give birth to another... such is yours my friend."

-Ali Hussein

"Bell's book dares you to do something most people hate: spending time alone with yourself. Going Alone addresses the very real insecurities most people think about. Once the lights are off and you're lying in bed and the cell phone is peeled from your hand; we think about: choices, regrets, and our untimely (but inevitable) meeting with death. Bell suggests not running away from such thoughts, but towards them, head on, preferably in a wilderness environment.

Where it's just you and The Great Indifference.

Even if the book doesn't motivate you to get outdoors, Bell's reflections on the desert, the meaning of a good life, and how to obtain a sense of objective virtue will be enough to lay the book down, take a moment...and listen."

-Giuseppe Rastelli

"It is not good that man should be alone."
-Genesis 2:18

WARNING

Do not go alone to the wild unless you are willing to accept the very real risk of suffering and dying alone. Take some precaution to let others know where you will be, and when you will depart and return. Bring something to save your life, such as a first aid kit, and a satellite GPS phone or emergency beacon. Again, do not go alone unless you are willing to accept the very real risk of suffering and dying alone, and are willing to accept responsibility for bringing pain to those who love and care about you.

~

Also, this is not a book of answers. Read on only if you are prepared to continue life with less; and are ready to die expecting nothing more. If so, then welcome to the result of my own *Great Life Adventure*.

"*Be you still, be you still, trembling heart; Remember the wisdom out of the old days: Him who trembles before the flame and the flood, And the winds that blow through the starry ways, Let the starry winds and the flame and the flood Cover over and hide, for he has no part With the lonely, majestical multitude.*"

-W. B. Yeats

Sections:

INTRODUCTION

How the journey began

*"If you want to live in peace,
go to the interior desert."*

-Macarius the Great

Greetings from a man in the past, with a sincere interest in your future.

My name is Kurt Bell. I am fifty-three years old as I write these words, which is important and relevant, as I do not think I could have written them at any other age. This book could not have been produced in my forties, or in any decade prior, or to follow. This is a story to be told from my fifties, and my one chance at describing the landscape and perspective of my life, as seen from this particular vantage and time. This is my *Season of Philosophy*, which is my way of describing a period of life for recording ideas and stories which are reflective and cumulative of the best lessons so far lived and discovered. This book is an effort at sharing my experience and advice with those to come, and who might be inclined to sit and read a bit from an aging man who will be gone from life much sooner than he'd like. For, despite my various trials and challenges, I do dearly love being alive, and it saddens me to know I will soon die and pass away forever to nothing. Saying this is not a forecast or prognosis of eminent death, but instead, is simply a sober reminder of the reality that life so often ends when we least expect, and sometimes just when we are at last ready to live.

I wrote this book with the young in mind, particularly, the young who are just now waking into adulthood with questions about the life they've found themselves living, and the future which yawns ahead like a strange road to uncertainty. I was in this same position once, from about age fifteen to forty-five, which was a long time of seemingly aimless drift. I'd like to help you shorten this period; and make better use of the precious days I believe we each only get once.

It took me a long time to break free of life's drift; and settle into what I call *a life of courage, joy, and independence.* There is no gimmick here. I have no ulterior motive. I do not believe in an immortal soul, and therefore have no interest in saving mine or yours. However, I do sincerely want to be helpful, and I'd like to help you enjoy a better life; and begin living this better life sooner. I will not ask you to believe anything I say, though I will explain the reasoning behind the arguments I propose. Let me start by sharing a little of my own background, and some of the events which contributed to the challenges I faced; and have mostly overcome.

I arrived at young adulthood on my own. At age fifteen my family was in the process of breaking up, and I was operating as an adolescent without much adult guidance or oversight. I was lucky though that a high school teacher at the time introduced me to a book titled Walden, by the author Henry David Thoreau. This happened after our English class had been assigned to read The Call of the Wild, by Jack London, and I had expressed to the teacher how much I'd enjoyed the story, especially the narrative description of wilderness, and the experience of life in the wild for both man and beast. I remember this same teacher taking time from her duties to walk me to the school library to locate and offer me a copy of Walden, which proved a pivotal event in my life, as the book opened my eyes to a way of living and thinking which closely aligned to some inner interests I was barely aware were developing within me. Walden helped me to find the courage to venture out and alone onto my own road, to...*follow the beat of my own drummer*, as Thoreau would describe, and to allow myself to live life in better accord with my own inclination and native aptitudes. It was the *going alone* bit which moved me most, as this provided an example in courage to strike out without companionship, aid, or comfort; and to take risks I might not have otherwise taken. I took Thoreau's example to heart; and began my own solo meanderings and living in emulation of a lifestyle I thought well suited to who I was, and the man I wanted to become.

My first attempts at Thoreau's lifestyle were a few solo hikes into the mountains surrounding our humble ranch near Lake Hughes, California. My family lived then in a very rural location, on ten acres of land a few miles up Pine Canyon Road from the community of Lake Hughes, sixty miles north of Los Angeles. Our home was surrounded by chaparral wilderness; and going alone required very few footsteps from our front door. I spent much time then walking alone in the wild; escaping perhaps from the confusion of my teens, looking for something, not yet ready to discover what *wasn't* there in the wild to meet me.

The remains of our home at Lake Hughes are still there, burned out after the fire which destroyed everything in 1983. The foundation and remaining bits of our lives at "Moonshadow Ranch" are located on the north side of the road, down in the river wash, just a quarter mile downstream from the remains of an abandoned highway rest area. Though our home site can be easily missed, the roadside rest is still evident by a dirt turnout and parking area on the north side of the road, amidst a cluster of tall pines.

Our family bought Moonshadow—which included a simple, one-bedroom home—for $15,000 dollars in 1976. We bought it at the tail end of a family journey we called "The Odyssey," when our traveling home was a converted Frito Lay potato chip delivery truck, and we wandered the United States and Canada searching for our collective selves. It would be a mistake to overlook the influence The Odyssey had on my life, which in many ways played as important a role in setting precedent for the importance of adventure as Thoreau's model of independence and self-reliance at Walden.

After The Odyssey—and after I gained the relative independence of a driver's license and a car—I began venturing further out on my own, even transforming my first car—a 1970 Camaro Rally Sport—into a miniature motorhome. I did this by removing all but the driver's seat, and fashioning a bed, dresser, and storage cabinet into the places where the removed seats had been. When I was done, I had created a little muscle-car motorhome, which was quite comfortable for my solo adventures; though honestly, I only used it a few times for this purpose. In fact, I found hitchhiking to be a more interesting and inexpensive way of getting around; and I was lucky to enjoy a short hitchhiking career before America lost its willingness to pick up strangers by the side of the road.

I began hitchhiking during the last two years of high school, initially just in California, though gradually I made my way halfway across the USA, and up nearly into Canada. I enjoyed three or four very long solo hitchhiking adventures during this time, when I literally went with the wind, and slept out in the open, with very little money, resources, or access to communication. These experiences (mini-Odysseys, really) had a great influence in dulling my apprehension about going alone. Today, I can thank those hitchhiking trips for development of the nerve and gumption I would later need to simply walk away from the sane and secure, to venture alone into wild places without a map, a friend, or any certitude regarding finding my way back. This early life path I was on—of ever extending adventure, of going further and deeper into strange places, always alone, and seemingly without a safety net—would likely have led me to disaster, and perhaps an early death, or a solitary life of social irrelevance, if it hadn't been for the institution of Chaffey Community College in Alta Loma, California, and a professor named David Bixler, as well as the small band of college friends with whom I shared a few years between high school and university.

David Bixler introduced me to Biology, as well as the more academic side of Thoreau, and the perspective of natural history, and the methods and processes of science; and gave me and many others our first experiences of true wilderness. David Bixler awoke the grown-up empiricist in me; and sent me forward on a life of reasoned discovery, with an eye and an interest in the frontiers of what we know, and why we should care about what is true, and not just what is comforting, traditional, sanctioned, or popular.

Another important event at this time was discovering the public broadcasting TV series, Cosmos; written and hosted by Carl Sagan. This program—and its companion book—won me over to the full paradigm of science; and ignited a flame of interest in the natural world which burns as strong today as when I felt my first shutter of awe at the recognition of deep time, and the processes by which our species has come to know ourselves and our small place in the universe.

The path I chose as a young man was risky, as *going alone* is a hazard at any age. Go too far...and you may not get back. And even if you return, some essential part may be left behind in the place you found; a place in mind, a place alone, a place you may never successfully relate to others who have never been so far afield without the comfort and guidance of maps, compass, companions, or gods. Going alone is key, and the people who visit deep solitude may appear eccentric or even mad to those who've never been; describing realities which don't seem very real; which may, in fact, only be real in the world they alone know. I sensed early this risk in going alone; and took measures to protect myself from going too far or too long. The most significant decision was my choice to settle and marry a young woman whom I love, respect, and admire, and who represents and lives a life very different from anything I had known. Likewise, was I to her. And together we formed a symbiotic union of stability and adventure, which has served us well for over thirty years.

Over time, I finished high school, went to college, got married, pursued a career, paid my taxes, and raised a family. I have managed to fulfill most of the expected roles and responsibilities of a social man of my time. On the other hand, I have also lived another, quite different life; a life in pursuit of the noble goals suggested by Thoreau, the example of the Odyssey, and the fond remembrance of the solitary adventures of my teenage years. Through this other life, I discovered and developed a separate side of myself, became the man whom Thoreau suggested I might be, and lived a life which has been a source of much satisfying personal fulfillment.

I wrote this book in appreciation of Thoreau's Walden, and other similar books which have influenced me over the years, and which I have identified at the end of the book in the Recommended Reading section. I hope my book may prove helpful, particularly to the young; to someone like myself, who finds themselves suddenly awake and conscience in a universe of wonder, and not sure just how to proceed, or how to best spend their time. I will not tell anyone exactly what to do, though I will share objectives and principles which I have found helpful. Nor can I offer companionship, as the path I recommend isn't wide enough for two; and must always be found and followed alone.

Now a note about how this book was written, the characters within, and the formatting approach. I wrote Going Alone between 2013 and 2017, between the tail end of my family's life in Japan, and the start of our new life in the USA. The book was compiled from various on-line journals, which in turn were composed in bits and pieces, via tweet-sized sentences and paragraphs—"blurbs"—which I pecked out on my mobile phone. I wrote nearly everything while on the move and adventuring, usually while walking and hiking, often far beyond the edge of Internet connectivity. Each upload was hash-tagged with a theme, which in turn became the major sections of this book:

#MymuseisaCorpse
#ThePathofWildness
#GoingAlone
#TheGoodLife
#TheStoicLife
#MygodisaLittleGod

The blurbs are rarely related, though sometimes there is a small story being told in the process of updates, which may become clear if the blurbs are read in their original order of upload. It is possible to find the original blurbs—in their original order—along with any associated photos, as well as date and time stamps, by referencing my various Facebook pages. In particular, my Facebook page softypapa[1] which is the place where nearly all of my extemporaneous writing did first appear. The blurbs are included in this book in italics and collected in sections under the heading "Notes from my muse."

The section of this book titled *The Path of Wildness* was developed while my family and I were living and raising our daughter in Japan, in the small village of Yada where my wife grew up. The Path of Wildness was my first try at the larger book. However, the story was not complete then, the ideas not fully considered or fleshed out, and it took returning to America, and my time alone in the desert, to complete the tale.

The section titled *The Anxiety Hike* is from a blog post[2] (and video) of the same name and was added to provide a guide to anyone who might want to experience for themselves, the landscape and inspiration for so much of this book's content. If you decide to try this hike, just remember to go alone for best results. Though keep in mind that the landscape here will kill you; and is incapable of shedding a tear.

My book includes some characters such as *the muse*, the *Ghosts of Siberia*, *The Soulless Beasts*, *The Desert Killer*, and *my little god* (deliberately lower case). These characters are, of course, fictional, and were created as foils to my own reflection on the character of humanity's encounter with something I call *The Great Indifference*, which is defined and described in the sections titled *The Cast* and *Going Alone*.

Place names are nearly all made up: *Black Mountain*, *The Deep-Water Wilderness*, and *Volcano Wilderness*, as well as places like *The Sandman's Bed*, *Mt. Wildness*, *The Woodsman's Cabin*, *The Edge of Deep-Water* and *The Home of Faith* are my own names for places without a name, or which I renamed for my own purpose. *Siberia, Bagdad,*

19

Black Ridge and *Campo #1* are real places, some of which are described well in Joe De Kehoe's excellent book The Silence and the Sun[3] which shares the history of settlement along the stretch of railroad and Route 66 between Barstow and Needles in the Eastern Mojave Desert, where much of this book was written. The stone-lined footpath at Siberia is real. Please be careful to not disturb the stones if you go looking for it.

I sometimes refer to "Biology" as though it were not simply a branch of natural science, but almost some entity or quality of our nature. In fact, I am using this word as a label to describe our innate drives and motivations, particularly those which are a result of our genetics. I use Biology where others might use the word instinct; though my meaning is intended to be more comprehensive, and reflective not only of the qualities of our being—which are the result of our DNA programming, including epigenetics—but also the possibility of more comprehensive programming by our society, upbringing, and times. There is some "Biology" in the behavior of an ant colony which cannot quite be nailed down to any particular genes within the individual ants. It is this emergent quality of groups, and society, which is somehow rooted in what we are, yet nevertheless transcends the individual. This is what I mean by "Biology." The sum natural qualities of what we are at the level of the cell, organism, family, community, and civilization. This is probably as close as I will get in this book to anything mystical or spiritual, though I am confident even the mystery of the programming of groups will one day give way to the inquiry of science.

My only regular companion in the desert is my 2004 BMW R 1150 GS Adventure motorcycle, which both delivered me to and from the desert, and kept me entertained with pleasant distraction when the deep void of nature triggered a response of panic or despair, and I ran. The desert is the perfect environment for this type of bike, which is branded a dual-sport adventure tourer, capable of both street and light off-road riding. Though I never rode it far off road—preferring my two feet for such travel—the bike was nevertheless ready for any dirt road or double track I chose to follow, and I could not imagine these adventures with anything else. What follows is a list of items I carry with me, or on the bike, to facilitate my desert adventures:

KURT'S IMPERFECT ADVENTURE KIT
Equipment and tools for desert travel and survival

- 2004 BMW R 1150 GS Adventure motorcycle + gear
  - Steel side panniers
  - Full windscreen
  - Fog lights
  - Schuberth G3 Pro modular helmet
  - KTM Powerwear motorcycle jacket (this jacket doubles as my heavy winter coat)
  - KTM riding pants
  - Riding gloves
  - Spy Riding goggles
  - Rain outfit (jacket and pants)
  - BMW USB power adaptor
  - Tool kit and tire repair kit + tire inflator
  - AAA Premium roadside coverage (100 miles tow)
- 5.11 Rush72 backpack
  - Large drop pouch (to hold bread for sandwiches)
  - Two (2) rock climbing carabiner to hook things on
- REI Half Dome 2 tent + ground cover sheet
- Outdoor Research Helium Bivy (for emergency overnight away from base)
- Marmot Trestles 15 degree sleeping bag
- REI Stratus Regular inflatable sleeping mat
- Clothing

- REI Vented Explorer's Hat (all year)
- Wool cap (winter)
- Medium-weight jacket (winter)
- Medium-weight vest (winter)
- Heavy sweater (winter, early spring, late fall)
- Light sweater (winter, spring, fall)
- Windbreaker (all season)
- Insulating long-sleeve shirt
- Heavy-duty button-up shirt
- T-shirts (2)
- Underpants (2)
- Hiking socks (2 pair)
- Heavy boots
- Hiking shorts with accessory pockets
- Strong leather belt
- Cooking Gear
  - Coleman 5 Piece Aluminum Mess Kit
  - GSI Outdoors Collapsible Java Drip + filters
  - Primus Express Stove
  - Jetboil 100-gram propane bottle (2)
  - Metal cup to boil water in
  - Metal clasp to pick up hot bowl and cup
  - MSR Alpine Spatula (collapsible)
  - GSI Outdoors Glacier 3-piece cutlery set
  - Lighter (2)
- Water Containers and H20 Rations
  - Platypus Big Zip LP 2.0-liter pouch (1)
  - Hard plastic 2.0-liter water bottles (4)
  - Cold weather: 2 or 3 liters per day
  - Warm weather: 3+ liters per day
  - Hot weather: Are you sure you want to do this?
- Lighting
  - A large flashlight for night hiking
  - Black Diamond headlight
  - A tiny light to carry in my pocket for emergencies

- o   Glow stick (to find my tent during night hikes)
- Emergency Gear
  - o   Small first aid kit
  - o   Moleskin blister dressing
  - o   Mobile phone (to use when in range)
  - o   Space blanket for emergency cover
- Food
  - o   Dehydrated ration (full meals, enough for the trip)
  - o   A loaf of bread + peanut butter & jelly (light meal)
  - o   Coffee and snacks, such as granola, chocolate, etc.
- Camera & Phone
  - o   Canon Ivis HF G10 video camera
  - o   Canon Directional Stereo Microphone DM-100
  - o   GoPro Hero Session 5 + floating hand grip
  - o   Sena Prism Tube helmet camera
  - o   iPhone 6s (32 gigabytes)
  - o   Otterbox Defender iPhone case
  - o   Otterbox lightning USB cable
  - o   External charger
- Beach Gear (yes, I bring beach gear with me to the desert*)
  - o   Bright red swimsuit (like a lifeguard might wear)
  - o   Mask and snorkel
  - o   Churchill bodysurfing fins
  - o   Beach towel
    * I bring beach gear as I sometimes will end a desert journey by riding to Shaw's Cove in Laguna Beach for a refreshing ocean swim. I usually go straight into the water from the steps (watch out you do not step on a stingray—ouch!) and then swim to the rocks at the right side (north) of the cove. If you look closely, you can find a little underwater cave which you can swim through which is an amazing way to punctuate any desert adventure.
- Miscellaneous

- o Hand towel
- o 50 SPF sunscreen
- o Journal/sketchbook, plus something to write with
- o Swiss Army Knife
- o Geology hammer + safety goggles
- o Spare batteries
- o Accessory bags & TP

So, here we go. Welcome to my book, and the result of my life's effort of fulfilling the suggestion and challenge offered by Thoreau in Walden. This book is my own answer and homage to that great author's masterpiece of expression of the bold experiment he made of his life, and the example he has become for so many. In 1998, I visited Thoreau's grave at Sleepy Hollow Cemetery in Concord, Massachusetts. While there, I left a small pebble atop his resting place—as had so many others before me—as simple homage to a man and his creative effort which has meant so much to me, and has helped me to be stronger and more courageous in my desire to...

"...live deliberately, to front only the essential facts of life, and see if I could not learn what it had to teach, and not, when I came to die, discover that I had not lived." [4]

Now, I leave a somewhat larger pebble to Thoreau in the form of this book. A simple gesture of appreciation for the *life of courage, joy, and independence* which I have found by way of his example.

Siberia ghost town

THE CAST

Characters, places, and concepts within my book

"What an immeasurable limitless desert this is.
What could you deduce here of God's purposes,
what, in this dead emptiness, is He permitting?
In this blank terrain, inimical to life,
all-consuming, all-consumed, totally burned up and out,
totally unsupportive of humanity's self-belief;
this fragment, or segment, of a world-self that is not;
this corpse which, never since the earth was born,
has given its creator a single word in return."

-Henrik Ibsen

Let us begin with an introduction to the places and characters
which play a role in my story of Going Alone. Some of these
will figure notably in the book, while others are only mentioned
briefly, or not at all, or may only appear elsewhere, such as in
my other writings or within the many videos I have made and
shared about the deep wilderness settings which I have
explored in Japan and America. Each of these places and
characters are important to me for their use as landmarks,
symbols, or analogy to the ideas I wish to convey; and as we
proceed through this book, I would like you to imagine four
separate regions where these places and characters exist as
elements of the story I want to tell.

The first region is this civilization we enjoy and share (even if you and I are separated now by vast space and time) and which is the common bond between my writing these words and your reading of them. I do not think I need to speak much of this civil place and circumstance between us, given the fact that it is our common human heritage, even if I am from California and you are from Istanbul. This shared resource of human connection is something we both know, enjoy, and may sometimes struggle to find and maintain a place within. It is our civilization, and our community, and our people, and our home. This is the place from which we will start. It is the setting out point for this adventure of *Going Alone*. Do not lose sight of it. Never forget what it is, or how important this grounding will always be to the well-lived life, to the social life, to *The Good Life*.

The next three regions of potential exploration are settings increasingly removed from civilization; places elsewhere and far away, distant, and remote to our common understanding and the comfort of what we know is true. You and I are both aliens of a sort in these less explored places, especially when we go alone, and especially when we go alone where there are no roads, trails, paths, or opportunity of help; or where the connections, security, and comfort we've left behind are now truly out of reach. At the near edge of this vast and mostly universal wild there is a crossing over point and borderland which I call *The Edge of Deep-Water*. It is a high point between civilization and the deeper wilds. A place where we can at once see, hear, and otherwise perceive both the last vestige of our home and community in the near distance behind us, as well as the empty lands of *wildness* dead ahead and down below. This, *Edge of Deep-Water* is someplace we can indeed visit. And if we are lucky, and if we go alone, then just maybe we will catch a glimpse there of the terrible thing I call *The Great Indifference* which is defined further in this book. I recommend going no further than this edge if you are timid or scared, or not willing to risk, or to lose, or to die seemingly too soon. This is my very real and sincere warning to you. I am not trying to seem dramatic or to simply entertain you with dangerous-sounding cautions. Death and something possibly much worse can really find you when you perceive *The Great Indifference*. Do not go alone to *The Edge of Deep-Water* if you do not really want to know. And if you do go, then go alone, and do not try to follow me... You will not find what is not there if you do.

Next, and beyond The Edge of Deep-Water, comes the *Deep-Water Wilderness* itself. This is where most of the remaining characters and places in this book are found. They are landmarks, as I said, and though they are indeed real, it does not really matter if you find them. In fact, you are better off discovering such things in a "desert" of your own seeking. Go somewhere else. Find something else. Take your own scary risks. Do not seek the places and things which I have found and have related here. Do not look for The Great Indifference just where I found it, as it will be hard to see with the echo of my past passage blinding your view and confounding your footsteps. And if you do go where I once went, and then successfully locate any of my landmarks, such as *The Watcher* or *The Miner* or *Campo #1*, or *The Home of Faith* or even *Mt. Wildness* itself, then I bet you'll stand there and say to yourself..."why the hell did I come here?!?" and "What was Kurt talking about? This is nothing!" And so, it'll be...nothing, to you. That is because, even if you went to my places all by yourself, you did not truly go alone.

The last place on my indistinct map of regions is *The Great Indifference* itself, which is both beyond, and within The Deep-Water Wilderness. It is everywhere, in fact, only we can see it better the further we get out there in the "desert." It's in the mountains too, and in the sea, and where you work, and where you live, though you can't very well perceive such empty in these places due to the clutter of life and the artifacts of living. To perceive The Great Indifference clearly, you will need a desert, and you will need to go far. Far beyond your own Edge of Deep-Water (give one last look back before you proceed), going down and into your own Deep-Water and then beyond. Do you see it out there? If so, then now what... Read on to learn how I answered this peculiar question in my own life, which is the substance and subject of my book and story.

But first, let's meet the cast of Going Alone:

Siberia Ghost Town

"Alas, how is't with you,
That you do bend your eye on vacancy,
And with th' incorporeal air do hold discourse?"

-William Shakespeare (Hamlet)

Siberia is a small, deserted community halfway up the Mojave Grade between Amboy and Ludlow in the Southern California desert. There is nothing at Siberia now but ruins and ghosts, and even these have only enough remembrance to barely exist as rubble, dust, and fiction. Come here when you are ready to go further. But do not expect to find what you are looking for. It is not here. True, there were once people, lives, and dreams at this place—lives and dreams like yours and mine—though there is nothing more now to see at Siberia, though there's perhaps much yet to discover and learn. But only if you go alone. And only if you find your own "Siberia."

BNSF Railroad

Siberia ghost town owes its existence and history to the Burlington Northern and Santa Fe railroad, the tracks of which run just north of the crumbled stone ruins of the ghost town's former train station. While nearby Route 66 has all but died, the BNSF remains a thriving concern, with mile-long freight trains passing east and west several times every hour, day, and night, breaking the desert silence with thunderous locomotives heading up a long string of heavy freight cars moving slowly through the desert. The locomotives proceed always on their way through every desert town and siding (even the ghost towns), by issuing four blasts of the lead engine's deep, resonant train horn: two long blasts, followed by a short blast and then a last long bellow as the train approaches and then passes through the lonely Siberia railway crossing. These trains are an irregular timepiece and reminder of what we have left behind in coming here. They pass us by very closely, yet remain impossibly far, especially at night, especially when there is no moon, and the wind blows, and we wake up, and we ask ourselves why we've come at all to such a place, and why we came alone.

Route 66

Route 66, aka "The Mother Road" is now a lonesome stretch of highway running alongside the BNSF railroad through much of the East Mojave Desert. This old highway is my access to Siberia ghost town...with the infrequent traffic along this road being but an echo of the millions of people who arrived in California via this famous and historic transcontinental thoroughfare. There is a marker facing east at the north side of Route 66, where a small dirt road leads off along the short drive up to Siberia. The marker is a large tire with the words "West Siberia" written on it in white spray-paint. I sometimes wonder how many west-bound travelers on Route 66 even notice the marker... Sometimes, I will stand a short way off in the desert near the tire to watch folk's faces as they drive past the ghost town entrance. The only people who ever seem to notice the sign—or me, standing alone in the empty desert—are the employees of the BNSF railroad, passing by in their large white utility trucks. They notice me as I am out-of-place in a landscape they know. The others never see me. They do not know this place; as they are perhaps too focused on their Route 66 journey, which is simply yet another unworthy distraction.

Siberia Bridge

"Active in indolence, abroad we roam
In quest of happiness which dwells at home:
With vain pursuits fatigu'd, at length you'll find,
No place excludes it from an equal mind."

-James Elphinston

This is the place where my muse lives—or where she followed me to before I at last caught up... We have conspired a lot down here...the two of us...as if we are truly just one. Such an idea! The bridge was our shelter, and a catalyst to thought away

31

from a reality masking the quite stark and terrible truth it took me fifty years to find. I have some personal things stashed down there in the rafters under the bridge: a chair, a camera tripod, and some chalk. You're welcome to these things if you find them, as they are a bother and a clutter to the simplicity that I first found here under this old road. The underside of this bridge can be a scary place to go when you are alone—especially at night. I would not want to go there if I was not already me. If you do go, well, you know...*go alone.*

The Path of Wildness

"The bounds of knowledge marks, and points the way
To pathless wastes, where wilder'd sages stray."

-John Courtenay

The Path of Wildness is both a place in fiction and something real. I first developed this concept while living in Japan and while exploring a wilderness landscape too civil and tame to reveal the deeper truth I would later come to know in the wilder places of the American desert. The Path of Wildness is symbolic of our courage in moving forward along the riskier courses of life, where such direction seems the way our intuition suggests we should go. It takes great courage to "step upon the path," which is a way untraveled, uncertain, and unforgiving. Yet, the rewards are sometimes—though not always—worth the risk, especially to those who no longer seek the gain. But of course, we can go this way only when we muster the courage to move forward alone. As there is no Path of Wildness to be found while in the company of others. Do not go if you are very scared. Please consider this my warning—

as what you might surely lose along the way may not be worth the journey. That is your loss.

Throughout this book I refer sometimes to paths, trails, ways and sometimes roads. I use these words carefully and deliberately. I use them to describe passage through life which is safe or sane or familiar or perhaps alien and strange and remote. Trails, ways, and roads are places where we follow others and where we are not likely to encounter anything which our species has not already met. Such places are seemingly tame and civilized and somehow sanctioned by virtue of the past passage of others—even if that passage was long ago and forgotten. Even the slightest hint of another of our kind will spoil the way, but only if you do not want to find what might otherwise be there. When we step off any road, trail or way and begin moving—preferably walking—alone, then we disembark from the comfort and reassurance of precedent. We leave behind our guides. We forget to follow. We begin to move on *The Path of Wildness*.

After returning to America in 2014, I discovered that The Path of Wildness in fact exists, as a short, stone-lined walkway in the empty desert surrounding the deserted ghost town of Siberia. You can go there and walk the path now—leading from nowhere to nowhere. Only do not expect the journey to end where you want, or where the path peters out, or anywhere in particular at all. And for best results—only go alone.

The Sandman's Bed

"But desert space and atoms invisible."

-Lucretius

This is a place I discovered during the *The Anxiety Hike* and
which is described in the chapter of the same name in this
book. *The Sandman's Bed* is an area of rough badlands made
of decomposing granite, furrowed by a maze of flash flood
channels carved into the granite through eons of weathering
and erosion. The area is immense and often without
wind...with very still and silent air...and an almost unsettling
quietude. The sand within the twisting, bone-dry stream beds
here is soft and easy to walk on, and while the loose and
weathered granite surrounding these dry watercourses is solid,
it is nevertheless slippery like marbles and slick like glass and
thus potentially quite dangerous to cross. This is a place where
you are likely to trip and fall or twist an ankle or pull a tendon
and become unable to walk. This is also a good place to come
to meet, and get to know, the side of yourself which maybe
didn't expect a universe without intrinsic meaning...or that
didn't know that you could be so lonesome with the idea of a
universe chock full of empty. Do you think you can weather
the silence here? Can you maintain your equanimity in the face
of such unsettling peace and quiet? Dare you take off your
shoes when you are so far alone into the Sandman's maze, to
then lie upon the sand, and close your eyes, and see just how
long you can keep your eyes shut. Come here other than alone
and you might as well have never come at all.

Mt. Wildness

"A fool's eyes wander to the ends of the earth."

-Proverbs 17:24

Mt. Wildness is my perennial destination, and a place where I have never been, and will never, ever, arrive--at least you'll never hear that from me. I made up Mt. Wildness while living in Japan; imagining this mountain as the home of the true things I feared most, and a destination I could strive for in my better moments. I imagined Mt. Wildness as having two sides: the near and the far side, with the near side being the place I could actually approach in relative safety, while the far side is an impossible distance I might indeed someday reach, but from which then I might then never fully return. Mt. Wildness became a real place to me after I came home to America and identified a very remote mountain in the Eastern Mojave Desert as this likely peak. I later concluded I was wrong and have since identified a new and much more distant peak— further and more terrible—as the "real" Mt. Wildness. It is my goal to hike to this mountain before my life is done. But I'll never tell anyone what I find there. Going to Mt. Wildness may be the last thing I ever do.

The Woodsman's Cabin and Campo #1

"When I'm there I hate it.
When I'm here I miss it.
It's a paradox."

-David Hempleman-Adams

The Woodsman's Cabin is another place which I dreamed up in Japan. The idea probably began as a result of the many abandoned farms—and in particular the forgotten and dilapidated old farm sheds, chock full of old farming tools—which I found while exploring in the deep mountains of central Japan. There was something about these deserted places which suggested past care and concern by humans, and the subsequent loss of any consideration or remembrance even. There is an emptiness about such places which in some ways is deeper and more telling than the mere nothing we can sometimes—and sometimes only—sense while alone in very wild places. This is the atmosphere and character of *The Woodsman's Cabin*—a token of the wonderful warmth and love of what was—discovered in contrast to, and within the cold embrace of, the emptiness which will forever be.

Campo #1 is a very real place, and the remnant of a former desert mining site located at the edge of The Deep-Water Wilderness. It, and the Woodsman's Cabin, are central to the story of Going Alone, as these real places are the last real frontiers of connection in my own adventure before entering a place, I call *The Valley of the Soulless Beasts*, which is too distant a place to visit in this book. I sometimes use this lost camp to overnight at when exploring the deeper desert. It is a good place to rest and sleep and remember what we are now, and what we soon must not become.

The Deep-Water Wilderness

"But what must be the solicitude of him who should be wandering, among the cracks and hollows, benighted, ignorant, and alone?"

-Dr. Johnson

This is a real place—though the name is one I came up with myself. Honestly, I do not know what this place might be properly called, as it seems at once too unremarkable and uninteresting a landscape to be worthy of a name all its own. But I gave it a name, nonetheless. You can get to the Deep-Water Wilderness by first going to Siberia ghost town (just plug the ghost town's name into your device's map application). After you arrive, start walking towards those low hills to the north. When you get there, then get ready...for what is beyond those hills is harder than it looks. That "beyond" is the *Deep-Water Wilderness*. Are you ready for a swim beyond your depths? Just how long can you tread and keep your head above water? This is the landscape where the *Desert Killers* live. The *Killer* is there when you expect it should be; but also, perhaps when you might not. The only real sanctuary here is the *Home of Faith,* which I have defined and described a little further in this book. But even faith cannot keep you alive or intact if you are too trusting, bold, or foolish. The Deep-Water Wilderness is someplace you should never bring any such nonsense. You have been warned.

The Edge of Deep-Water

"Therefore the door of death is never closed to sky and sun and earth and sea's deep waters. No. It stands open, and with vast gaping mouth it waits for them."

-Lucretius

This is where you can fairly safely go from Siberia, if you simply want to glimpse the empty without much risk of the empty glimpsing you. Never go here during summer though, as you really will not make it back. However, during almost any other time of year, just go to Siberia ghost town and then walk north for a mile or so until you reach those low hills. Carefully climb the hills, and when you reach the top then look north out over the edge. If you go to the highest point in these low hills, then you can stand in my own footsteps for whatever that might be worth. I wonder if you will also feel my fear while you stand there. Look north and down now from where you are. That place down below is where the last part of the Anxiety Hike took place. You are standing now at the very final point in the Anxiety Hike chapter of this book, at the place where I point out that you can see Siberia once more...you can finally see safety again! You are out. You have made it.

There is a *"Watcher"* down there (described below) in that twisting canyon just below you, watching even now, even a hundred years after I write these words, down and a little to the east. Can you find it? I have left something there for you in case you try. Though the Watcher is watching always, it will never see you, as there is too much empty blocking the view. If you are lucky, then this same empty will soon become apparent to your own view—this is *The Great Indifference*, which begins here. Those black mountains dead ahead—yet very far—in the distance...that is a place to go. But remember always, the Desert Killer which can easily find you from this point on. There is a sanctuary here called *The Home of Faith*. Can you find it? I never did. And I died without knowing. Just like my father before me. A very worthy death—if not without some risk.

The Muse

"I sat down to make notes on a green bank, with a small stream running at my feet, in the midst of savage solitude, with mountains before me, and on either hand covered with heath. I looked round me, and wondered that I was not more affected, but the mind is not at all time equally ready to be put into motion."

-Dr. Johnson

I first learned of the muse through literary references, though "she" did not start speaking to me (or at least I did not begin to notice or hear) until my early to mid-20s. At that time, her voice was more youthful and optimistic, full of new promise, and hinting at the rich and varied life of potential to come. Was she fooling me then? Or perhaps was she simply as young, dumb, and innocent as I? Our work product together then was an expression and outlet for a rich fecundity of thought both buoyant and light, and characterized by an animate energy that was my right at so young an age... Now, my muse is older, and seemingly more mature. Her attitude is still one of optimism, though she tempers this with an almost cold and naked inflammatory confession that she was never alive to begin with. All those years of warmth...that was simply me embracing myself in the mirror; holding my hot mortal being to myself, while pretending there were two of me: myself, and my muse. Now, I know there was never the muse, and it was always just me... And now I feel my end is coming soon. And for this reason, I no longer lie. The muse is nothing. Her impression is my own want of something more. Her inspiration, my vain expression of lasting substance and eternal life where there is none. My muse is a corpse. My own corpse. A recognition of death before I am dead. And a decision to live while there is still some time left to be alive.

The Ghosts of Siberia

"The graves are very numerous, and some of them undoubtedly contain the remains of men, who did not expect to be so soon forgotten."

-Dr. Johnson

These ghosts were suggested by the presence of graves I've discovered at and around various ghost towns in the Eastern Mojave Desert. Though Siberia ghost town does not have a proper graveyard, there are nevertheless a few stone monuments which appear to be graves, scattered here and there in the surrounding desert. These markers suggest the memory of people who once lived here, and who made this place home. These are the "ghosts" which haunt my thoughts whenever I come here alone. Remembered, in fact, by no one.

The Great Indifference

*"Is there none out there to respond? No one at all?
No one in the abyss? Nor under the heavens' shell?"*

-Henrik Ibsen

This concept is central to the entire story within this book. *The Great Indifference* is the book's last destination, and someplace from which I have conspired an escape. That is the somewhat hidden punchline of the story...that we can meet something in nature so awful as The Great Indifference and then carry on living good and meaningful lives without either denying or hiding from the fact of what we've not found; or making up stories to dispel and quiet our fears. The idea of encountering The Great Indifference is that when we go far enough alone into nature, we may discover a type of emptiness and void which is both awesome and unsettling. It is this vista of disinterest which I call *The Great Indifference*. It is a recognition of no love or caring in nature beyond what we find with one another, as well as with a few select species which have evolved to become our companions and friends. Other than with these, there are none who truly care if we live or die, thrive, or suffer; or if we even find peace with the wholesale recognition of just how truly alone, we really are... In short, The Great Indifference is the recognition of a universe devoid of the wishful presence of a loving god—or any god—or any others, besides other members of our species or our pets, who might have some capacity to love and to care. The Great Indifference is a place utterly silent of evident meaning. It is also suggestive of our own capacity to create meaning by our

41

own willful decisions and efforts. To reclaim some sense of meaning from the awful night.

"Only the solitary individual is subject, like a thing, to the fundamental laws."

-Rainer Maria Rilke

Disclaimer: There is a problem with this term *The Great Indifference,* in that the phrasing suggests some context or character from which indifference might *emerge*—namely, it suggests god; and I do not mean that. In fact, I mean the exact opposite. I perceive no god out there in the deep desert. And the arguments others make for god being real are clearly weak, and contrived, and poorly reasoned; constituting little more than a thin veneer of pretend, masking the necessity of faith to hold aloft ideas more vacuous of truth than fiction; more empty still for the very fact that believers accept the fantasy as true. And the irony, that I created a term to describe a universe seemingly *devoid* of god, which then winds up backing me straight *into* god (it may be a deistic god, but a god nonetheless), does not escape my attention...and honestly, this fact frustrates me a bit. It is a problem of language. An issue of vocabulary. As I cannot quite find a better term or phrase to describe the universe's seeming uncaring or incapacity to care, without then also implying something with this very capacity to care. I will live with that.

Another problem with the term *The Great Indifference* is the fact of us... We are part of this universe, and we are certainly not indifferent. In this way, the universe has indeed acquired the ability—through us—to become either interested or

42

indifferent at least insofar as we, and other sentient species on earth like us, exist, and through the possible existence elsewhere in the universe of other forms of sentient life. In this way, the universe is clearly not indifferent. Yet, it seems that the vast infinitude of the universe does mostly match my original meaning of *The Great Indifference*, insofar as this term describes what I perceive—through my quite limited sense and cognition—to be an enormous vista of emptiness and uncaring, which serves as the backdrop and context for every aspect of our lives. We avoid staring into this deep empty by way of our incessant busy living, punctuating our moments with innumerable distractions and entertainments. And in living this way, we fail to see what *is not* out there not loving or caring about us, in fact may not be *capable* of loving or caring about us, or even knowing that we are here. And by ignoring this great emptiness and void we then run the risk of perhaps attributing more to the universe than might be warranted; dreaming up fantasies of significance and eternities of joy for the good and damnation for the bad which the universe mutely implies are hardly real or even utterly false. So, I will stick with my term *The Great Indifference*. Partly because I cannot think of a better phrase, but really because it's exactly what I'm trying to say.

A few times in this book I reference a place called the *Volcano Wilderness*. This is a place about thirty miles west of Siberia along Route 66 and near the town of Newberry Springs. This is the very first place I spotted—and almost recognized—The Great Indifference. To get there simply drive to the end of Gasco Road and park near the fenced gas pipeline work yard. Do not worry, nobody is likely to bother your vehicle here. Get out and begin walking south and uphill toward those low black mountains in the distance. It is a long walk. A very long walk.

43

When you reach the mountains, then find your way up and to the left. When you arrive at the top then look over the edge. That thing you do not see down there...that is *The Great Indifference.* But do not bring anyone with you unless you are only after a difficult hike. This is also the area where I brought my daughter, and where I found those human bones mentioned a few times in this book.

The Soulless Beasts

"Man that is in honour, and understandeth not, is like the beasts that perish."

-Psalm 49:20

A class of animals—which include me—who wander the desert wastes beyond the pale memory of what once was alive and loving at and around Siberia ghost town, and other desert places like it. *The Soulless Beasts* are strong, and full of the base energy and determination which characterizes nature in places which humans have forgot or never cared to love. The Soulless Beasts typically emerge at night—being most active in moonless dark—which fact hides their living; and camouflages their determination from any minds which might suspect something more to life than simply staying alive and getting our genes into the next generation. The Soulless Beasts display both purpose and meaning, of a sort, while trotting, crawling, slithering, or flying along *The Path of Wildness.* I know what it is to move among their midst. I know when I am with them alone what it is like to have no soul. I remember that I too, have no soul.

The Desert Killer

*"For all things soon pass away and become a mere
tale, and complete oblivion soon buries them."*

-Marcus Aurelius

Death stalks the desert lands at all times; though most
particularly during the very hot and very cold seasons, when life
can be either burned out of us from within or evaporated away
in the shivering cold. In either case, the killer does not care
about anything we might feel, or say, or do, or pretend while
our living is slowly drawn out and away through either an excess
or absence of temperature. Death then, is nearly always present
and persistent in the desert. Death never cared nor cares.

The *Summer Killer* lives in the east, and arrives at dawn,
and stalks the wastes boldly throughout the day after mid-
morning; retreating only at night; and sometimes not even then.
The *Winter Killer* comes from within, though its breath is the
cold outside night wind; and its touch, the caress of cold outer-
space looming with empty behind a thin veil of breathless
atmospheric night. Beware these two killers wandering the
seasonal wastes. Avoid their paths. Stay clear. Your death is no
matter to them. They are not real and are incapable of care
regarding life or death.

My little god

"All men are equally afraid of death when they see it; only some have a power of turning their sight away from it better than others."

-Pasquale Paoli

My little god is so small as to be almost non-existent. He lives with me to remind me of the things I fear and which I am tempted to invent solutions for in order to make the fear go away. My little god gets angry when I doubt, or ask questions, or consider other options. He wants me to follow him—though he has no real idea where to go; and would rather sit at home all day or even hide beneath the covers of my bed. I make an effort to write his name "god" in lower-case letters, though if he could read, he would surely see this as my sacrilege. I do this to him as a deliberate insult to his feigned importance and contrived consequence. It is an expression of my disdain for his petty, mere, and very slight existence. An existence only within my mind, and when I think of him, and when I call his facile cheat.

I have made a home for my little god there in the wilderness. It is just below the Edge of Deep-Water. Below that place I previously suggested you go, to look across and over the place you should probably not go.

My little god is very real. He came with me from Japan; and lives now in a small hole above that sandy wash leading into Deep-Water from the dangerous abandoned mine shaft. Check the holes. If you find him...if you find my little god...then tell him please that he is not true—and then leave him alone there, to become forgotten once more.

The Howling

"He found him in a desert land,
and in the waste howling wilderness..."

-Deuteronomy 32:10

The Howling represents the place which is further and beyond the point where I know I can venture, and still hope to return home sound and intact to my family. It is not that whatever is out there making the howling can necessarily hurt me—though it certainly isn't harmless—but instead that once I reach that place, I can probably never fully return. Something of me will remain there always, or will die, or will become extinct—like a lost memory of something that once was and will never again be. So, while I have no plan to discover the source of The Howling during the course of my otherwise sane and sober living, I do hope that chance will allow me one last fleeting glimpse before the final light of my living is extinguished for good. I do not think I can successfully hear or locate The Howling unless I'm very, very alone.

The Watcher

The Watcher is nothing more than a pile of stones atop a small rise adjacent the southwest flank of the hill I call Black Mountain. This name "Watcher" came about after I first spotted the stones of which The Watcher is made, during one of my earliest hikes in the area. I'd been about a mile away at the time; and could see atop the rise what appeared to be a solitary human figure standing and looking my way. This sight was quite unsettling at the time, as I was convinced, I was alone there, and could not imagine another human being anywhere nearby, let alone someone so clearly watching me. The figure never moved though throughout that first day, and I soon determined it was nothing more than a pile of placed stones—probably a mining claim. Return visits to the area confirmed my suspicions, as The Watcher was always there (he's probably out there now) and when I at last paid him a visit, I found the site was indeed nothing more than a long-forgotten pile of stones marking the site where a miner had once suspected some mineral riches might be found. It is interesting to know that the stones which the miner so carefully placed here remain still in their assigned positions, so long after the hand which set them has certainly turned to dust.

The Miner

The Miner is the last—though not the final—character I've so far met within the Deep-Water Wilderness. You will find him sitting atop a small ridge about a quarter mile from the spot where the canyon leading up from the dangerous abandoned mine shaft begins to open and widen into a landscape of color (see the section of this book titled "The Anxiety Hike"). The Miner is there, off to the right, maybe not looking at you, in fact—perhaps looking at nothing—but there, and looking, nonetheless. I would imagine this miner might be the last familiar figure I'd see in this life should I someday find my end out there "*Beyond Deep-Water*", in the heart of the black mountains, or maybe amidst the Sandman's Bed, or perhaps even out there somewhere in the distant vicinity of Mt. Wildness. This is not an end I want—though it is also not an end I would not want.

The Homunculus

"Ay, but to die and go we know not where;
To lie in cold obstruction and to rot;
This sensible warm motion to become
A kneaded clod..."

-William Shakespeare

The *Homunculus* is nothing more than that little man or woman who lives in our heads, and who peeks out at the world from behind our eyeballs. It is the small person who pulls the levers and pushes the buttons of our mind, guiding us along and steering our body and brain through every circumstance and decision. The Homunculus is the one who suffers when we fail, who rejoices when we succeed, and who stands accountable for every consequence of the fact of our life. This little "person" is trapped in our head, cannot get out, and will die when we die. The Homunculus sometimes fools itself into thinking it can, and will, one day escape our cooling corpse. It tells itself that there is a way out, a hatch somewhere perhaps to admit it away from the end of our mortal being. The Homunculus has no idea where this hatch is, nor any clue about how to undo the binding straps which hold it secure within our cranium. But never mind these facts...it will survive. We simply know this is true. Though we have no idea how or why. Some Homunculi though, prefer not to be fooled. And they look out at the world, not as a temporary passenger prepared to embark to somewhere new, but instead as a trapped and bound mortal, counting down the months, days, and hours to an untimely end. Untimely, insofar as it wants to go on...but knows it cannot. For this reason, such Homunculi are sometimes reluctant to close their eyes... Why sleep now when there is still some light? Why rest when there is yet living action to perform? Why die when there is still some possible time to live? This is *The Homunculus.* The little mortal within our head. The one little life we get to live. A life and living of one. A very true and real example of *Going Alone*. But only if we recognize there is no apparent way out.

The Home of Faith

The Home of Faith is a dark and quiet place... There is little sound or sunlight here, where the stone walls are as thick as a mountain, and the darkness within the cave as deep as any hole might expect to get. The way in is easy... Just decide to believe instead of pursuing doubt...and the portal will open, and you will stumble or fall some impossibly near distance into a dark depth you can hardly comprehend. It is then very hard to get out, even if you do find an exit. Once inside, it is tempting to continue retreating further until the disturbing noise of reason which sent you here becomes silent at last. Then—once you can no longer hear—you will be satisfied, though you will also really be quite alone, alone with your confidence, which shines with only the dimmest cold light. There is no real warmth here, though there is a sort of comfort...a comfort you can get used to over time. The cold comfort of *faith*. This is after all... *The Home of Faith*. Beware that. It is the same comfort of the grave... Linger here too long, and you too may become just another living, buried corpse.

"These are the furnace-lands
These are the burning wastes
The apotheosis of desolation
and solitude
Rocks and thorns, baking
Under a lunatic sun
A lizard scrambles, alarmed
By the shadow of a circling
hawk
This arid wilderness, thick
with ghosts
Where mad prophets wander
And the jinn gyre and dance
The empty promise of water
In a wavering, distant mirage
I came here to this place
where all hope dies
A lonely, forsaken death
I came here, like I always do
For this is the wellspring of
imagination and thought;
My harsh mistress muse
Hunkered down, under this
bridge
My refuge of shadow
My fortress of silent solitude
I stare out at the glaring day
And wait for inspiration or
madness
Either one is good."

-G.L. Stokes

Where my dead muse lives

THE WRITING BRIDGE

Where I wrote the story

"We must go alone. I like the silent church before the service begins, better than any preaching."

-Ralph Waldo Emerson

Siberia ghost town in the East Mojave Desert is flanked on the north by the BNSF railroad line, which runs east and west through a great expanse of otherwise quite empty desert. On the other side of the ghost town—running parallel to the railroad—is Route 66, or the "Mother Road" as it is sometimes called. Both corridors of traffic—rail and road—have existed here, in various forms of improvement, for more than a hundred years. I first found Siberia ghost town after spotting from the road, the lone, standing stone wall which now serves as the center of the empty community which once was. I noted the wall while driving eastbound on Route 66; probably just as I was driving over the bridge which would later factor so significantly in the tale of the writing of this book.

I certainly did not notice the bridge when I passed over it that first day back in 2015. I was simply exploring the East Mojave by car, moving slowly along Route 66, checking the road on either side for anything of interest for potential exploration. In fact, I wasn't looking for anything near the highway in particular, as I wasn't much interested in anything too close to the civilizing touch of either the highway or the railroad, and I was instead searching for good places where I could safely park my car some distance away from the road, while I went for a long desert hike. So, when I saw the ruins of Siberia, I wasn't drawn to these for their own sake, but instead to the fact of a relatively well-maintained, short dirt road which left the highway leading to what appeared to be the ruins of a very old building. "That'll do!" I probably said as I flicked on the left turn signal and made my way carefully off the Route 66 asphalt and onto the dusty road.

The distance from the highway to the ruins is about the length of a football field. Not far at all. And the dirt road is in good shape, seemingly well-traveled and well maintained. I would later learn that this was due to the ongoing attention of the railroad workers[5]—track men, signalmen, linemen, railroad police and others who make their living keeping this stretch of railroad in safe, operational order. I would later come to know some of these men. Swell guys. Honest, hard-working men. People I respect. And I always strive to stay out of their way when I am at Siberia, and never allow myself to become a nuisance to their hard, honest labor. In fact, I have found labor here too, of a sort... Though I am never paid for my efforts, Siberia has become a quite effective work site and source of inspiration for me for both my writing and my videos, as well as my every effort of improved living. The ghost town—and in particular, the bridge under the highway near the town—are where my desert muse does seem to live and reside. Live, despite the fact my muse is quite dead and non-existent, a figment of my imagination, alive, in a sense, only as long as I live, and have the will, and the way, and the motive force to breathe life into something only my own musings might create. My muse did find me here in the desert, in the ghost town of

Siberia. She did then also follow me far out into the desert where she mostly shadowed my movements, nearly always silent, refusing to speak to me among the holy relics of the dead mountains and forgotten wastes of a landscape that never cared, and never lived, and never knew, or loved or possessed any dear sentiment, thought, or capability which our species might attribute to life. My muse was my unloving, unfeeling, unthinking and unliving, imagined escort though a place where I could never pass without her attentive ministrations and silent whispered hints of something more to be found beyond my adventures and excursions, something to be found in the place I'd left behind; in a life I must love should love ever be anything to dissuade the emptiness it was then too late to unsee or forget. The muse is my desert voice. A silent soliloquy and homage to what I can never truly know, or share, or escape from. My muse resides and originates from under that desert bridge.

So, what part does the bridge at Siberia play in all this? Was there some poetry to be found beneath the girders and beams holding up the highway? Did the muse follow me from somewhere else in the desert (or Japan) to that place in the shade beneath the road? Does my muse live there still while I am away? Can the muse be found there after I am gone, or if someone ever came with me to the desert? Why the bridge? What role does that place play in this story? Shade and shelter are the answers. A refuge from the heat and fury of the desert summer. I came to the bridge out of necessity—and then discovered a place of catalyst for what I might immodestly call my art.

The first time I went to the bridge I did so simply to get out of the sun and escape the heat. The heat. So impossibly intense there in the deep East Mojave during summer. There is truly no rest from the blaze in the open desert. The sunlight out there can surely kill. So much energy piling on across whatever skin is exposed. A real threat. Nothing to take lightly. So, on a very hot July day in 2016, I decided to pack some water and a few necessities and hike the quarter mile to the nearer of two bridges which I could see supporting Route 66 to the east and west of Siberia where flash flood arroyo crossed under the road. The first time I did this I went to the bridge to the east of Siberia. It is a good bridge. And I found some interesting things below it; including a travel book, written in Japanese, with a hand-penned note (again, in Japanese) on the back. The note was written by a man who declared that "he would not die away from home" and that he "would make it back alive." I went back to that bridge again a few months later. The Japanese book was still there. The shade was good there. It was a fine place to rest and find shelter. The bridge served well the important purpose I was then after.

It was not until a year later before I tried that other bridge—the bridge to the west. I decided to visit that other bridge when I realized the western bridge was closer to the Siberia ruins than the eastern bridge. The fact of being close was good, as it allowed me to better keep an eye on my motorcycle parked back at the ghost town ruins, which I periodically check on by popping my head out from under the bridge to make sure nobody is loading my bike onto a truck or setting a match to the gas tank to create a desert bonfire.

There was also something good about the space below the western bridge (though there is not much head room down there), but there is also something more... The sand is very soft, and good for sitting. It is a good place to plop down and think. And that is how the writing got started... Just sitting on the soft sand below the bridge, with the sun roasting the desert beyond my shade, and the sound of periodic automobiles crossing fast overhead, and the frequent rumble and growl of mile-long freight trains moving by slowly a quarter mile to the north. This setting under the western Route 66 bridge became my place at Siberia ghost town... A sort of circumstance and atmosphere where I could cultivate and get to know better the muse I'd met earlier out there at the edge of the blank desert wilderness. A dead muse who seemed willing and able to follow me sometimes to the places where I go, and where I am willing and able to think. To think, without much distraction I cannot willingly ignore. To think, where the conventions of my kind and the ways of our collective consensus appear as weak sentiments easily put aside in favor of whatever else can be proven more sound and compelling. This is the bridge where I wrote much of the content found within Going Alone, especially the content under the heading "Notes from my muse." This is the bridge where I discovered the solution of developing a life of meaning in the face of a universe which seems so far devoid of intrinsic meaning or purpose beyond the mute scope of survival, and the worthy act of passing our life from ourselves into those who will soon take our place. This is the home of my desert muse. And the place where I found the words of the story I do now choose to tell.

Let's Start...

There's a wilderness behind this page
It's someplace invisible to some
Evident to others
Beautiful to a few
And perhaps deadly to anyone,
Who can't find their way back

I've left some signs within to a way out
It isn't easy,
But then, what's worthwhile rarely is

I did not write this book
To lure you to death,
But to show you a way,
A way to good living,
The way I found,
A way which works

No magic is necessary,
No trust
No faith,
Just courage
And resolve
And a will to live

So, turn the page now if you're curious,
Come *alone* to a very real place,
Leave your treasure behind,
You won't need it
Where you're headed now

The Homunculus

MY MUSE IS A CORPSE

Sensing we are alone

"The world's broad, bleak atmosphere was all
so comfortless! Such, indeed is the impression
which it makes on every new adventurer,
even if he plunges into it while the warmest
tide of life is bubbling through his veins."

-Nathaniel Hawthorne

This section of my book chronicles the three-week experience of having my desert inspiration follow me home to the city. I had no idea how long this "muse" would stay, though I'm glad I could record a little of what it had to say. This experience began on March 4th, 2017 and was complete on March 23rd.

I have enjoyed a long relationship with my muse, which tends to arrive suddenly, urgently demanding I record my thoughts before she withdraws, and leaves me with nothing more of substance to think or say. I first met my muse in my early 20's, while living alone for several years on an empty stretch of beach in Northern California. The muse would meet me sometimes at night, while I walked alone along Moonstone Beach just south of Trinidad, watching the sea glide up and back across the gentle shore slope, expiring in shallow, sweeping wet sheets, the last energies of powerful waves crashing loudly in the distant dark. I would walk then with my "moondog," which was the name I gave the reflection of the moon upon the wet sand, glistening with a brilliant cold pale light, following me everywhere the earth was wet. A loyal companion in her every phase.

The muse has since been with me always, through every decade of my life, speaking via the mediums of poetry, prose, art, and video. She visits at her leisure and pleasure, though I have found that activities such as walking alone, listening to music, and the moderate application of alcohol have a way of luring her out—though she never stays for long, and if I fail to listen, or write down what she has to say, when she's saying it, then her message will surely be lost. My muse will never speak to me in the presence of others, though sometimes I detect her voice when I read good books, or hear interesting people talk.

I have never fooled myself into thinking that my muse is anything more than my own creativity. I know there is no supernatural entity visiting me with inspiration, and I'm aware that this creativity is subject to my own circumstance and well-being, and that my muse will die with me, or perhaps one day falter and grow silent when my mental energies which now produce her begin to fail (this process has already begun) or my will and interest shift to elsewhere or no place at all. Thus, the urgency to write when the muse speaks. Thus, my desire to share before both she and I grow silent and are gone.

The following words are the product of my muse, spoken to me at odd times, requiring I step aside from work to write down what I hear, or pull my motorcycle to the side of the road to do the same. They tell a story in a way, in bits and pieces, ideas strung together over time, revealing a train of thought buoyant of life, cognizant of death, and catalyzed of action. I am my muse's shadow author, though she and I both know she never really exists.

Notes from my muse

It's flattery to call my muse a corpse, as she is so much less; having never been alive, she has no still heart, no snuffed out conscious, no darkened lattice of memory, and certainly no legacy of love and caring to echo through time in life's wake. I call her dead by means of convenience, to call attention to what she has not, to highlight how far she is removed from the dearest possessions of life, and to enshrine her grave indifference with the startling, fearful aspects of what cannot possibly love, and has more in common with sand than the buoyant, striving, animate community of life.

~

My muse is blind, deaf, mute and dead. She is the inorganic fact of reality. The inanimate ambition of entropy. The chill, dark waste between the stars. The uncaring substrate of physics and chemistry; bound, secured, and destined towards some emotionless mathematical end.

~

Crossing now from the place where I share life with humanity, into the vast void of indifference. At once I find my own voice again. At last, the muse returns.

~

Yesterday's long desert sojourn was a new experience of indifference. A recognition that the cold shoulder of nature is made of stone.

~

Yesterday's desert hike left little impression at the time. Almost a disappointment, in fact. Yet in hindsight I re-see those far and empty places. My thoughts come back to them over and again.

~

I'm haunted by this past weekend's hike like no hike before. I'm pretty sure I went further than I should. Deeper than I thought I could. My reward, the deepest draught of indifference my mind can yet withstand. Such an awful, fearful, terrible truth.

~

My muse is a nihilist, whispering cold words describing the eternity of empty beyond death. She'll meet me only in lonesome places, like a conspirator or a thief. But really, she's a confidant, and perhaps my most honest friend; though she laughs at my fear, and mocks my every vain hope.

~

It's curious how the muse was nearly silent during my adventure last week in the Deep-Water wilds. She normally only talks to me when I'm alone, and at risk, in very wild places. Instead, she followed me home this time, to whisper barely audible thoughts throughout the week; touching my shoulder during meetings, suggesting ideas during my commute, smiling at me through a distant crowd. I wonder how long she'll stay? Why she now talks to me here? What brought her in from indifference?

~

It seems my muse did not follow me back from the wild to inspire my words, but instead to catalyze my will. How much easier to do right while hints of the void and empty swirl behind my head, and memory of the black mountains of indifference loom across the wasteland of dry earth.

~

The thing which followed me out of the wild this week, which I've been calling my muse, isn't a ghost, or a spirit, or a force or anything beyond the scope of my mind. It's simply a lingering impression, the sting following a hard slap in the face, the cold, deep, indifferent reality of nature. A lasting effect of meeting the dead gaze of a universe which doesn't care, doesn't feel, and doesn't know. I hope this impression lasts.

~

Almost went to the wild today. I decided instead to attend to a few domestic life necessities. That's alright. It's not like wildness gives a damn if I come to visit. The dead winds howl across the Indifferent badlands, against and over the cold black mountains, through and along silent sand washes, to twist and bend the dry, thorny foliage, with or without my attendant, failing gaze.

~

The melancholy peace, of a solitary walk in the deep desert, has found footing in my everyday sojourn. The dull, dim, yet alert and living eyes. The sensitive hearing. The slow, purposeful stride towards nowhere in particular, along unseen and unmarked paths. And best of all, the rich and empty

66

thinking which comes of lonesome, yet not lonely, passage through strange, unpeopled places.

~

A principle of deserts is that winds blow into their depths, and point the way towards deeper desolation, and the arid, disinterested heart of the wastes. While standing upon a broad open plain at night, invisible mountains miles distant on either side, their outline visible only by the interruption of starlight through the cold, thin atmosphere, a slight veil between the bare, stony ground and outer space, I shiver alone and cold, feeling the dead desert breath draw me in like a tide.

~

The scope of my control extends to my actions and reactions, and the consequences they might entail.

~

Death is the realization of that creeping indifference which sweeps consciousness and being aside like fallen leaves, and carries both memory and love along into the darkened night.

~

To the quiet mind, indifference looms. No wonder then our myriad and incessant manufacture and attendance to distraction.

~

The deep value of a solitary desert walk is the sobering recognition of a landscape and circumstance without any real escape. For though we may return to our warm bed and our fellows; the memory lingers of the cold night winds under the naked stars, and the blistering sunlight across a vast landscape without refuge. Such impressions gain deep footing and purchase within the mind, but only when we go alone, and only when we go so far as to glimpse the very real and near point of no return.

~

To a mind which has risen above fortune, both the necessary and superfluous actions of the day become like attendance to a disinterested game of chess. For while our mind and body must periodically engage the game and move the pieces, our deeper attendance is to matters more worthy of our true character and aim.

~

Do you attend your dying breath in this present moment? How much more worthy a pursuit than philosophy. I'd rather reckon each exhalation, in deep fastidious awe, than the gilded words of the holy and wise. Indeed, if their wisdom be true, they'd silence their speech and mind in mute attendance of their own mortality, and the consequent vista thus revealed.

~

The fallow field of the well-lived life is the time between riches, fame and security. A time to cultivate a more true and honest harvest.

68

~

The price of leisure is attendance to the fact of who we are and the choices we've made. It's no wonder then we sometimes choose for ourselves the slave's abject distraction.

~

The sober subject of our life's decline arrives so often late to the feast, and long before the diner has enjoyed their fill.

~

There's a similar sensation of precious anxiety which results of descending forty feet beneath the sea on a single breath, or hiking four miles off trail into a stark and barren wild. But only if you go alone.

~

Not only the fact of humanity, but all trace or reminder of our race, must be left behind before we can truly sense there is no God.

~

Reason is the arbiter of virtue. What other force can provide a more accurate or worthy measure?

~

I have this plan which I'll never fulfill, for I am a family man and must respect the sensitive conscience of those who love and care about me. However, if I were alone in life, and

69

received my physician's forecast of pending death, and were to have this council affirmed by a qualified another, then I'd make provision for a last and final journey into the wild; the desert of course, to find my end in the wastes, alone and without succor, to face down indifference in its own awful light; stark and devoid, pale and blinding, cold and incapable of care. I wonder how I could handle such a last adventure? Could my mind bear with peace such a truth, even as the light and caring of my own being flickers and fades into the dark, cold void.

~

My muse seems lately at ease with her new surroundings. A transplant of the desert wastes to the living suburbs. Her mute voice speaks as always of her home in the wind and the night, remembers the empty badlands, the colored soils, and the unending progress of time. She looks around her new surroundings, dead eyes seeing nothing past the here and now; no regard for humanity, no love of virtue, or charity; no preference or admiration of what is alive or dead. No wonder she seems so at home...when I now realize she was here all along.

~

How like a hermit crab I have become... So insular and self-contained. My needs, of course, extend to society. Indeed, I'd die without my fellows. And I like to hope my fellows might need me in some small way. Though beyond the sustenance of my person, I find now ample nourishment for the mind and spirit in such dull pursuits as the marking of time, and the vain cataloging of the many treasures I am so fortunate not to possess.

~

*I had an interesting talk with a friend today where I confessed
my nihilism, and found comfort in not giving a damn. Such is
how the serpent consumes its own tail.*

~

*Hiking in the desert with my daughter is like sailing a boat
upon the sea with a long tether tied to the dock.*

~

*Emily and I visited the human femur I discovered in the desert
last year. It's still there, despite the fact I'd notified the police.
Maybe they didn't find it? Perhaps they gave up the search?
After all, the bones are literally in the middle of nowhere. It's
possible they determined the bones aren't human, though this
seems unlikely given the absence of large wildlife in the area,
and the perfect match to human anatomy. I was rather
surprised to note how much the bones had deteriorated since
my last visit. Further proof that our essence is essentially
animated dust. I plan to call the Sheriff's office again and offer
to take them to the spot.*

~

*It was strange being in the deep desert today without my dead
muse. Where could she have been? I suspect it's because I
didn't go alone. In fact, I know that's the cause. I did see signs
of her presence in the wind, and across the darkened
landscape, and in moments of subtle extrospection. Though to
hear her cold words rise within my mind I must remember to
first deny myself the warmth of any companion, and to face*

*fully and alone the fact of all mortal dissolution and oblivion.
Only then will the muse speak to me her mute inspiration.*

~

*Though my muse is not alive she nevertheless enjoys some
apparent will and motive force. Her composition is maintained
of gravity, and her limbs and appendages are driven of starlight
and wind. Her attitudes and moods are as varied as the
composition of rocks and soils, and her intellect and modesty
the product of vast space and deep time. Some very small part
of her does have an organic pulse, this is true, though this soft
rhythm is utterly drowned out by the roar and cacophony of
nature's inanimate rush towards entropy. Though my muse is
not alive, her words and law-like meaning nevertheless ring
clear in my brain whenever I muster the courage to look past
the warm company of fellowship, and the reassuring clamor of
minds, to the intense dark beyond the firelight, and the deep
abyss beyond life.*

~

*It's interesting how my daughter did not share my fear in the
wild yesterday. She seemed at ease in a place I've practically
run from in the past, that slippery granite mountaintop where I
first caught sight of the hidden heart of the Volcano
Wilderness. I felt an echo of that old fear yesterday as we ate
our lunch together upon that windswept peak, gazing over and
down into the place where my dead muse lives. I'm confident
her comfort was in part a result of our company, and I do
wonder what she might have thought or felt there alone, in a
place so silent my daughter at one time commented she could
hear her own heartbeat. Would the muse speak to her? Would
my daughter feign have never come? Does her young mind
perhaps require more years to better apprehend what isn't*

there in the desert wastes? Is it possible such absence simply goes unseen to those unfamiliar with its hollow circumstance and empty aspect?

~

My father's legacy. All those worries. At the bottom of the sea.

~

The wild places of the California desert have proven so much more potent a fount of inspiration than the mountains of Japan. I suspect though that this has more to do with the characteristics of desert than any condition of place or quality of time.

~

How blind I was to the desert muse before Japan. Though I could never find her voice while I was away in that exotic land, surer still her absence had I never gone. If I'd remained in Japan, my sight would have continued its myopic plunge into the familiar; the green and wet mountains and valleys there rising and widening in scale and contrived importance, ossifying at last into a world view of comprehensible dimension and satisfying importance. I would have at last died in my course there, satisfied of my living career, placated by my narrow world view; an invalid, comforted by my own deep ignorance. Since returning to America though, I face the familiar with alien eyes and foreign design. There is no more latent comfort in what was once all I knew. My weary eyes strain to discover the familiar. Old brain circuits crackle to life, mending failed, flawed or erred mental connections with material of another land and culture, values and meaning of a second and quite completed life. Tired limbs now become limber of the necessity of building this new life again, and old muscle memory is replaced with fresh reflex, guided of matured control and sensibility. It is with this reborn self that I have encountered and connected with my desert muse, found her fleeting across the wastes, utterly lost and invisible to the man I was, and was again; visible only now, as such a one as I could surely never meet or know over the course of just a single lifetime.

~

The faculty of choice is most keenly exercised at rough and unexpected life juncture. Does misfortune rise in our way? Does death approach? Is it not now in our power to exercise discretion and judgment in recognizing what is within our control? Have we not utter claim over our thoughts, actions and reactions? Do we not possess the ability to watch with equanimity as our fortunes rise and fall again, correcting our course with judicious turns of the rudder, aiming for the open sea yet breathing calmly as we become ruined upon the rocks and plunge beneath the waves? Our opinion and judgment of things lie outside the pale of all external forces besides ignorance, disease, and death, which may first weaken and then destroy our resolve and capacity to stand. But until that time we've power enough to select and will our own footing. To observe and recognize the vast machinery of the universe's headlong tumble towards tomorrow, and to know both the scope and scale of our meager influence.

~

As I have no one to pray to, I'll instead suggest an admonition to myself: Let my footsteps be slow today, to delay the world in its orbit, and force time to better measure and dispense its precious ration. Let my mealtime portions be small, let me

74

*endure the healthy want of food in proportion to my usual
excess. Let me then grow lean and strong as a consequence,
better able to survive, endure, and appreciate the true suffering
of those without. And let my thoughts be very few and small,
just some simple words this hour and the next—ideas sufficient
to my true need, or better still, my honest lack thereof.*

~

*What philosophy, maxim or dogma can withstand the scrutiny
of solitude in deep, wild places? In fact, if we linger too long
alone, then madness may steal the show under the guise of
sagacity. Be careful then to first uncover and refine truth within
the bustling tumult of everyday life, to then temper what is
found in the cold light of empty nowhere. Such understanding
then is forged of humanity, hardened of nature, and activated
of our improved subsequent living. Tell no one what you've
found, yet answer honestly every pointed inquiry.*

~

*How much better a retiring mind than a retiring body. The first
may be attained at any stage in life, at least so far our
philosophy permits. The latter only upon leisure, and the gross
accumulation of sustaining resource. Liberate the mind at once
through the discipline of reason, and you may then work hard
to the end of your days in contented leisure.*

~

*What number of individuals is required to tame the wild? Two.
No more are needed, though greater numbers are certainly
better to this end. No individual, no matter their will, resolve or
strength, can ever civilize even the humblest blade of grass.*

Only in company, or better still society, can this great feat be achieved.

~

What opportunity this? Does my leg ache? Fortitude. Does my neighbor complain? Patience and an attentive ear. Have I lost my job, or reputation, or security? Resilience and apathy. Does my life now come to an end? Resignation to facts, and a loving smile to those from whom I must now depart.

~

The penalty of actually incurring the risks which appear so present and fearful during youth, is less terrible than the punishment of their aversion, which must be sustained and borne when we are old, and our opportunities have passed. Youth is the time to assuage mid-life regret.

~

Occupied with distraction from cradle to grave, our lives pass with little notice or regard of the wilderness void which is our eternal, inanimate home. Our certain dissolution and apparent finality of being is masked with unreasoned promise of hidden tomorrows, filled with answered hopes, happy reunion and joyous reconciliation. We turn to death in our time, chanting "There is more. There is more!" while the evident nothing envelops us like a tide. Our deceived corpse, no longer capable of care, dissolves to matter and energy—our last, utterly conscious-less act, the slight tipping of the scale in the balance of entropy. How better, or perhaps more desperate, our lives, should we give up the unfounded myth that there is something more?

76

~

Tempered consumption forms a firm bedrock to philosophy. Observe appetite with caution, as you would any passion; sample it to determine if it is mean, base, or sound. If wholesome, partake less than you'd like; leave always the appetite wanting; become strong through willful resistance. If our temptation is unsavory, empty, or lacking in virtue, then leave it aside altogether—starve instead on a feast of fortitude.

~

Picking my way carefully down the mountainside. Did I really climb so far? Was it really then so steep? My declining thoughts are a mix of the inspiration of the lofty vision my progress had attained, coupled with concern about the darkness in the valley below, growing deeper with every minute, creeping slowly towards me up the mountain. Such a long day it's been. Such a fine day for climbing. How did I lose track of the time? Instead of photos now; I choose instead to simply think.

~

Credulity puts on airs with the feigned dignity of dogma and the false virtue of faith. Better to go through life without answers than to believe without good reason.

~

Very soon my life will fold in on itself and wink out like the dim candle it has always been. Yet my muse will remain. Being dead, and having never been alive, my muse has the capacity to persist beyond me. She will carry no memory of me besides the fading influence of my words and deeds. My muse cannot miss me, speak my name, or remember me to another. My anonymity is scarcely more secure in the grave than when my pulse was beating, and I had some voice to be known. My dead muse keeps perfect secrets; is incapable of telling truth or lies, is the perfect confidant.

~

I've declined to a place where my poverty is secure from fortune. I've so little of real worth that my desire for more is fully satiated. I owe no mortgage to reason, own outright my capacity to choose, pay no tax on apathy, and wield discretion like a sovereign. This outpost of peace was always near within my recognized ignorance. Easily attained though the journey required fifty years. I owe thanks to Seneca, Epictetus, Aurelius, Emerson, Thoreau, Sagan, Attenborough and Bixler for suggesting the way.

~

I've begun the process of watching an acquaintance fail in business. It's a venture in which he's likely gambled everything, and thus has everything to lose. I've been there myself, twice, and the memory is so real it's almost tactile. I laid up late last night staring at the ceiling, thinking of him. I'll bet he was staring at his ceiling too. Just like I used to do. Beginning to drown. Going down through a form of death which isn't really dying.

~

Apathy arms us with the same indifference which the universe wields in the execution of its mindless purpose. We stride through life bestowing benevolence in true proportion to our capacity; sharing unalloyed generosity and love, rich in the giving, expecting nothing in return.

~

Returning from solitary adventures in the mountains of Japan: the rugged landscape persisted in my head like an intimate and cloistered hideaway. The desert however, unfolds in the mind like a great and empty map; devoid of sanctuary, exposed and utterly impersonal.

~

The will of apathy is neither mean nor small attention, but freedom from undue investiture—to apply our focus and efforts wisely, to make good and useful ends of our days, to be a benefit to mankind, and not burn our energies over useless kindle and conflagration.

~

The optimist's bright luster cannot be dulled by apathy, nor their charity, kindness, or philanthropy. Indeed, these qualities are enhanced and made potent through a distilled and refined focus; the narrow and distinct possession of mind which comes of knowing what is—and what is not—within our own control.

~

Our true, and perhaps only, essential purpose is etched into our being with the imperative of desire, and the awful threat of living and dying alone. It's a mindless drive, truly requiring no thought. We live our purpose on auto-pilot; fulfilling its mandate with the satisfaction of every instinctual whim. An easy way to live, and a satisfying way to die.

79

~

Life is orphaned from the start. Our progenitor having more in common with a stone than the loving parent we might hope to deserve. We stand and gaze across the wild for some sign of kin and kind, our eyes drawn at last to the sky and stars in hazy remembrance of dim, indifferent origins.

~

We awake! Our fresh senses alive, and new, and electric with perception. At once we begin our locomotion; stepping and grabbing and speaking. We're never lost, not for a moment, though our minds may despair of purpose or meaning or direction or worthy end. Indeed, a deep mandate has the reins. A singular, worthy end. There's but one direction, one meaning that really matters, a consolidated purpose, driving and quite distinct. All artifact speaks to this one end. All else is abstract substance and substrate, compost and waste, filler and raw resource towards the gain.

~

I was asked today by a friend about my thoughts on the topic of worthwhile employ. Should the best occupation yield leisure and option to my heirs? Provide a catapult and catalyst to the next generation's situation and state? At the time I was asked, I thought such an aim both worthy and admirable. But upon some reflection I see now little good in laying up my days against the improvement of my heirs. For if the better aim of virtue is a mature capacity of wisdom, enlivened with fortitude, made lean and impervious of apathy, and grave of self-control; then how much better to offer our heirs, instead of wealth, the worthy example of our well-borne poverty, and the steady

80

resolve, and still motion, of a body and mind at peace with self-control.

~

How might I become impervious to well-being; develop an immunity to good fortune, and make the good life a reality despite every blessing.

~

My poverty cannot withstand the price of so much good fortune.

~

My tribe are those who currently stand among brambles, wondering how they got there, bleeding a bit from the thorns, observing no trail back. Perhaps a book like Walden sent them this way; though by now they've far less use of a guide. Indeed, what wildness is this that requires a guide; when every direction is in, and there's now far too few rations for retreat. My tribe will know this place, though none of them are about. They'll find me here long after I'm dead. I'll leave them some marks. I sometimes spot marks of those who have gone before me; faint, strange, nearly indecipherable the further I go. There are older marks still, appearing fresh as the day they were made.

~

What should I tell my child on the use of time? Should I caution her simply to be mindful of its passing? To measure each moment with her attentions, and keep busy with the application of sober utility? Should I recommend foresight towards the life she may want to live? If so, how do I caution

81

her not to reside too long in the fiction of what might be; or against setting up house in the past; or living as a ghost within the life of another? I must indeed offer caution against the waste of moments, which is the sport and pastime of so many; the impatient counting down of hours towards an ignoble, and seemingly, untimely death. Yes, I'll instruct her to beware all this and more; to mind carefully what is ahead, and what is passed; to not lose sight of her own way by ingracious attention to the footsteps of others; and to know her true and even course not by the landmarks of her surroundings, or the warmth of the air, or the pleasant company, or the ease of the road; but instead by the satisfying perception of firm footing over any ground, any fortune, and for as long as her daylight remains.

~

Our genetic inertia propels us towards ends we rarely consider: sex, love, marriage, and even Jesus proclaim our mute acceptance of responsibility to the survival of our species. Our blind allegiance binds this mandate to action. The veil may never rise for us, though the ones to whom we may one day become god should certainly pity our narrow vision, and quite constrained understanding.

~

Society bears down with a crushing weight of responsibility, while the wild bears down with the weight of necessity. The consequence of failure in the first circumstance may be destitution and disgrace, while failure in the second punishes with death and extinction. Going alone then into the wild relieves for a moment the first and lesser burden, in exchange for the thrill and challenge of a more base and primal threat. When we return from wild places alive, and mostly intact, our

82

perspective is changed and temporarily revised; for what threat really is any office censure; any mere social disgrace; an embarrassing fumble of etiquette; or even failure in love or enterprise, compared with what we've just met and mastered? The more consequent danger is now passed, and we move on through the day with a contented grace, having brought back a hidden trophy and prize in the simple fact of our survival. But this peace is perishable, requiring refresh at regular intervals lest we again mistake the civilized challenge of responsibility with the wild threat of necessity.

~

The human project is the occupation of attention until we've run out of time, death arrives, and we're no longer forced to perceive. Indifference is the thing we do not want. For if we quiet our mind enough, something which isn't really there becomes apparent. And if we separate ourselves far enough from our fellows, there it isn't again. To apprehend this startling absence, through dead landscape or still mind, is like sensing a ghost which isn't real; a frightening paradox to not behold. So, instead of not seeing, we first do this, then we do that, and then yet another thing; and then we die; hopefully well distracted, by the community and clamor of loved ones, whose presence and attention assure us there's more than nothing in the end.

~

Make your Great Life Adventure early in life, when you've both everything and nothing to lose. The gamble then is more secure in your favor, the likelihood of success augmented by your ignorance and inability to recognize or assess risk. You'll succeed even if the adventure kills you. Just don't get pregnant, and in so doing assume your own risk onto the life of an innocent another. *Save that wondrous adventure for later, when you've had your fill of yourself, and are more mature and ready to truly give. For your adventure's venue, select what appears alien and strange; a curious and seemingly foreign life street or some exotic backwater of nowhere. Go meet your anxiety, and give it a fair listen; rebuke its fearful claims and hysterical protests. Come away satisfied you know better your mind, and can now answer and assuage its ancient unsound fears. You'll know when the adventure is done, when you possess fewer dreams of tomorrow, and behold a broad and expansive landscape of today. Oh, and go alone...if you can bear it. If not, then take, or better still make, a friend along the way. You'll find your tribe is out there.*

~

Your mind is on a track. There's actually very little leeway between birth and death. The course is strikingly simple, though we don't notice due to our one chance at living, and the fact that our perspective biases us to exaggerate what little difference there really is between one life and the next, and one generation to the next. Gender plays a role in the course we must live, as does age, though these aren't very popular topics to discuss. But keep that in mind, and listen to what your nature has to say, even if you choose not to heed; for informed choice brings both responsibility and accountability into the hands of the chooser. Always apply reason to your Biology, always demand diplomacy of your motives, always seek virtue of your wants, or deny them altogether. In this way, never hesitate to resist your nature should it prove base, barbarous, unjust, or inhumane.

So, you'll bump along this course of living, fortune heaving you at once to the left, and next to the right; but always forward, and at a steady rate, even when at rest, even when you decide not to choose. Remember that you'll always be on those rails, and there's nothing spiritual or spooky or inexplicable about them; so, don't get suckered into motivation, divination or exorcism to change your way. Instead, ride the rails like the successful survivor you have become, we have become, we've all become, by virtue of the simple fact we're alive. You see, Biology's criteria for success is both simple and absolute. So, ride your rails to the end of the line. And if you choose, pass carefully your successful mandate into the future, as your mother and I have done through our loving creation of you.

~

It's been over a month now since my dead muse followed me back from the desert. She's always right here whenever my mind falls away from the fore. She lurks like a shadow and a memory, though her cold presence is now devoid of the fearful substance I remember of our first encounter. How my breath was taken away at that first sight at the edge of the Volcano Wilderness. I wonder if she saw me then too? Did she know me before? I certainly never knew anything prior so awful in the wild. Though there was that one cold night...thirty-odd years back. That night I passed alone within a vast desert empty, an empty which brushed past my tent while I slept, threatening my youth with its whispered age, and inviting me out to shiver barefoot and exposed while gazing up at the dark night, and across at the black empty. I was young then. Perhaps too alive to see. Maybe that's the reason she's here now? Are my eyes simply opened? Was she here all along? Will she ever leave? I think I know the answer. Though it's perhaps best I keep that supposition to myself.

~

How much is enough? For myself, it is enough to stop asking this question. For if my ethics are sound, my reason keen, and my intent judicious, then there will always be just enough of every endeavor. So instead of asking after the quantity of things, I should instead seek after their quality. How sound today my ethics? How keen my reason? How judicious my intent? Let me then tune my social machinations to run silent, efficient and true, satisfied that whatever product is the result, of whatever quantity, is utterly sufficient to The Good Life.

~

Where will you set up house? Though the body must reside in some shelter of a sort to keep it safe and warm, the mind needs only space and liberty sufficient to exercise its native capabilities and natural inclination. These places are not incompatible; though an excess of the former may indeed distract from the latter; while too much of the latter may cause disconnect from those who share our former.

~

Is it possible my dead muse has died? Is that even feasible? If not truly dead, she certainly seems less present. Perhaps it's because I've been so long from her dead home out there in the desert? Maybe the spell has simply worn off? She can't utterly be gone, as I hear her faint whisper now as I type these words; like a distant cold wind across a skeleton landscape of stones and sand; hushed and muffled; indifferent and absolute.

~

My dead muse is gone... The only words which remain now are my own. These thoughts are familiar...though they come with that same labored effort I've known since youth...like pulling a heavy root from hard soil. It was easier when my dead muse led the way, allowing me to follow behind as she stepped easily through abstraction, pointing the way towards silent impressions I cannot muster alone by way of my dull pedestrian life. I expect a trip back to the desert will secure our reunion. Though I wonder if she'll ever follow me back here again? Has she perhaps seen enough of civilization's vain and glossy proposals of meaning? Has she had her fill of our fearful efforts to hold back her night? The words are gone.

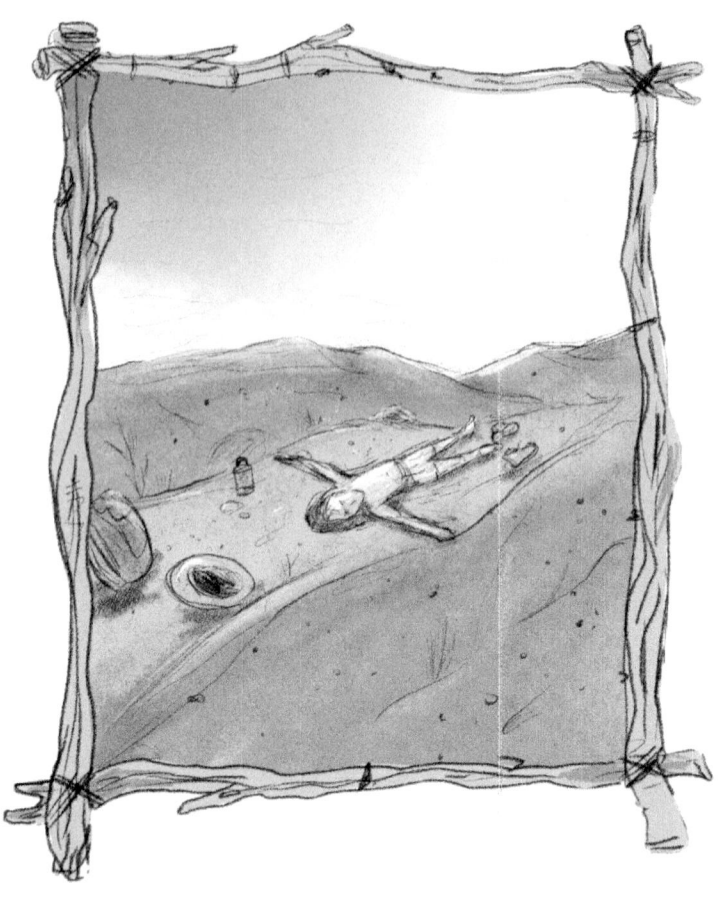

The Sandman's Bed

THE ANXIETY HIKE

Discovering *The Great Indifference*

*"Or will he, after the tomb-like seclusion of the
past day and night, go forth a humbled and
repentant man, sorrowful, gentle, seeking no
profit, shrinking from worldly honor, hardly
daring to love God, but bold to love his fellow
man, and to do him what good he may."*

-Nathaniel Hawthorne

Sharing the way

I am going to tell you now how to get to a place where I have
reliably encountered *The Great Indifference*, though I suspect
the very telling may spoil the way. If you follow my path, then
you will likely find nothing but sand, and waste, and heat—all
the composite bits of what you are after, without the substance
of what is not really there. My guidance is the problem... The
fact that you have followed my words to a place which I found
while alone, and in a sense, lost. You may need those alone
and lost bits yourself before you can find the indifference. Not
to be lost—in fact—but instead to be somewhat indeterminate in
your navigation, and knowingly off-course in your movement.

When you've reached the point where you've satisfied your
curiosity about the route I once took, then ask yourself if
you're ready to step off the unseen marks of my past trespass,
to embark along new lines towards your own solitary waste and
desolation. If ready, then put aside my maps and guidance;

stuff these deep into your pack or tear them up perhaps. But do this only if you've a mind to crush the empty promise of discovering anything of real value by retracing my footsteps exactly. So prepared, step now onto the soft sand, or across the hard and slippery granite. Begin walking where your feet will go. Do you have your GPS life beacon? Is it charged, armed, and ready to save your life? If not, are you willing to gamble deep and hard with your own soulless mortality for the chance to meet what isn't there in the deeper wastes? If so, then you do not need my words any longer. Go, and die today in the face of what is not, to continue on and better as part of what really is.

Hike stats:

- Distance
  Five miles round trip approximate. Return is via a different route. Actual mileage may vary greatly, depending upon how closely you fail in following my course, and how successful you are in losing your way.

- Trail quality
  There is no trail here, though there are many potential *Paths of Wildness*. The terrain is mostly flat, with everything rising on a slight incline south to north. The landscape is uneven, with hard and slippery granite and rhyolite slopes, periodic sandy flash flood arroyo and gullies, and several steep, black volcanic domes. There is little or no shade. You will be utterly exposed. And utterly alone. For that matter—and for our purposes— the trail quality here then can perhaps be honestly described as perfect.

- Best time to go
  November through April. Avoid summer months

91

unless you are truly ready to meet the *Desert Killer.*

- Dangers
  There are many: heat, exposure, snakes, spiders, rugged terrain, open mines, no connectivity, and no help. Also, there is no love or caring here—beware, these may follow you back.

- Reasons to go
  Solitude, history, natural beauty. To encounter The Great Indifference. To lose so much you never knew you did not need.

- Indifference rating
  High chance of encounter, but only if you go alone.

Why did I come to this place?

"...not in the soft obscurities of retirement, or under the shelter of academick bowers, but amidst inconvenience and distraction, and sickness and sorrow."

-Dr. Johnson

I am haunted by something which does not exist. Something which does not drift across the desert sands, or linger in the cold night air, nor touch my heart, nor press my words. Still the words do come, arising from my own forceful optimism, drawn along in their emergence by the vacuum pull of a landscape which does not and cannot care. The desert is indifferent to my ideas, my positions, my feelings and even my life. Though it can and will consume these, not through any action or intent on the part of nature, but by way of the landscape's withering neglect and disregard, and the resulting loneliness and disconnect which is the bittersweet end I always seek and discover in such places; as well as the very torment even my bones must painlessly endure as they dry, bleach, and crack to sand under the inferno sun, before desert winds then scatter what's left of me to oblivion.

A type of anxious motivation comes to me whenever I tread alone into a place which I sense is not just indifferent to my life and death, but incapable of even giving a damn about either. With some mischief I call this self-inspiration my muse; and reckon it a she. Such poetic license... I do worry that I am only confusing matters by not speaking plainly that my muse does not really exist. She is only a thing of my mind. A circumstance of place and time, and past experience, and disposition, and bias, and want.

Going Alone

"...but that it is easier to sail many thousand miles through cold and storm and cannibals, in a government ship, with five hundred men and boys to assist one, than it is to explore the private sea, the Atlantic and Pacific Ocean of one's being alone—"

-Henry David Thoreau

The words I seek, and which I attribute to my muse, come, in fact, from my own liberated senses. The experience is like the anxious freedom a child knows when they go past the limits prescribed by caring adults, to take thrilling risks which yield secret and suspect reward; and hold unknown and unforeseen consequences. The words which arrive to me in this state have more in common with fearful, mad laughter than sane and sober sagacity. Perhaps this is the reason I must always go alone. For to share this experience with another must surely break the spell of relentless risk and introspection. And

93

perhaps this fact can also explain a little why I sometimes fail at my efforts to enter the deep desert alone, and instead turn back for home, citing my family and responsibility and other worthy reasons to give up.

But hope is not lost for those who aim to find more than just my footsteps. All that is needed to go beyond my path is to simply not stop looking—to continue past the lines I've marked with my words; to trespass the unknown and uncertain; to be ready to fail, ready to become lost, ready to never come back. And most importantly, to be ready to go alone.

When to go and what to expect

"...but when they heard in their own voices the sound which tells a man crying in the wilderness that he is alone, they were silenced."

-Jens Peter Jacobsen

I recommend this hike from November through April, when temperatures are manageable and not too dangerous. Though beware the precipitous nighttime cold which comes on fast as soon as the sun passes over the horizon. Even in summer you can chill deeply through the night due to the limited cloud cover, which absence fails to insulate the Earth, and allows the accumulated heat of the day to dissipate quickly away to space, as from a bare body on a bed without a sheet.

As for heat, there is little shade anywhere along this hike, so dress appropriately, with proper protective cover and liberal application of sunscreen. The reason I did not include October and May in my recommended hiking months, is that though the morning temps at these times are quite nice, the afternoon direct sun can be blistering given there is no escape.

Particularly dangerous is the fact of occasionally—and surprisingly—very hot days during these months, which can easily kill anyone who goes too far, and finds themselves trapped in the rising heat, miles, or hours from safety. Do not let the blissful conditions of morning lure you so far into the desert that you can't escape when the inferno turns on at around 11:00 AM. Death is easy here, and it sneaks up quickly upon the foolish and unprepared. Even with sufficient water you may not outlast the experience of prolonged direct exposure to the relentless sun and heat.

Arrival and campsite

"There was not one who did not dread the moment when solitude should deliver him to the tyranny of reflection."

-Dr. Johnson

Siberia ghost town is easy to find... Just type: "Siberia, California" into your navigation app and follow the way. There are no amenities in Siberia—It's a desert ghost town after all—so be sure to get whatever you need at the community of Needles, Twentynine Palms or Barstow, depending if you approach from the east, south or west respectively. Do not be fooled by the fact of Amboy. As of this writing there is really nothing there of much help.

You will not need a four-wheel drive vehicle to get to Siberia, as the only dirt section of road is short, and passable by an average two-wheel drive car. When your navigation app indicates you are close, you'll see on the map that you must turn from Route 66 onto a dirt road which leads a short distance into the desert to what's left of Siberia ghost town. As you approach, look on the north side of Route 66 for a large tire propped up on a pole beside the entrance to the dirt road.

This big tire was placed here by railroad men who marked it with the words "West Siberia" (East Siberia is where the road crosses the railroad tracks) and who use the tire to help them easily find their way off Route 66 to the Siberia railroad crossing. I have also heard from the railroad men that the East and West designation are references to the direction of train travel on the railroad. Do not be surprised if you see one or two big white railroad trucks drive by during your stay, as this important and active stretch of rail seems to require constant attention. The railroad men have only rarely stopped to say anything to me during my visits here, and I don't think they mind much my nondescript little camp, or the fact that I routinely park my motorcycle near the ghost town ruins. To be safe, I recommend against parking or camping too close to the railroad tracks, or especially the crossing, or little signal shack, as this might indeed raise the attention of the railroad men, who must keep this line secure, and in continuous operation. Please also keep in mind that the area around Siberia is private property, belonging to the railroad for at least fifty yards on either side of the tracks. The railroad police do patrol this area, and they will not be too happy finding you near or crossing over the tracks. Otherwise, they seem to be fine with folks parking at, and hanging around, the area of Siberia[5]. I recommend leaving a note with your vehicle to inform the railroad police that you are hiking in the desert, otherwise they may mount a rescue party to go find you—as they once attempted to do with me, though I arrived back in time to stop their effort before the helicopter was airborne. Another landmark at the juncture of the dirt road is the enormous "Route 66" graffiti painted in white lettering directly on the ground where the Siberia dirt track meets Route 66. However, don't count on those painted words to be there in the future, as this stretch of Route 66 is long overdue for a repaving, and I don't expect the lettering to last should the California highway department come through with fresh asphalt.

When you near the big tire juncture, slow and then turn off Route 66 and onto the dirt road (watch out, as there is a sandy spot just as you come off the highway). You are now entering the remains of the community called Siberia, a place which once served travelers moving on both the railroad and the highway, as well as miners who prospected and worked claims in the surrounding mountains. This ghost town formally began life in 1883 as one of several water stops for trains on the Santa Fe railroad. The steam locomotives of that time consumed water greedily as they climbed westbound up the Mojave Grade from Amboy through Bagdad, Siberia, and Klondike (aka Ash Hill). Clearly, the names given these spots are suitably evocative of far and remote places, and harsh and hostile landscapes. And the names are appropriate, as you will discover when you visit.

When you arrive at Siberia, you will find a single crumbling stone wall marks the current center of the ghost town. This wall, and the foundation upon which it stands, is all that remain of the railroad station at Siberia. Though you can drive right up to the ruins, I recommend instead that you park your vehicle some distance away, as the dirt and sand around the ruins is littered with rusty nails which can easily make your adventure more interesting with a flat tire. I usually park next to the eastern edge of the dirt road which I drove in on (roughly parallel the ruins) and then set up camp a short way out in the open desert. If you look closely, you might even find signs of my camp, which consist of a rectangle of the large stones I use to hold down my tent ends, and a small wooden block (the end of a railroad tie) with a metal grating affixed to the top which is a table for my stove. Like all of the ruins at Siberia, it's likely my own ruins here will outlive me, and remain to perhaps provoke questions in anyone who finds them after I am gone. Again, when setting up camp, beware of old nails, broken glass and sharp, rusted metal in the sand which can easily puncture the bottom of a tent, sleeping bag, or you. I refer to this site as my "base camp" as I often use it as the setting out point for longer adventures into the desert.

If you arrive before sundown, then I recommend spending some time exploring the desert around the Siberia ruins, where you are sure to find many reminders of the town which once was. I suggest a walk through the desert along the dirt road leading back to Route 66, where—with a little luck—you will find the remains of a stone-lined footpath which someone created here decades ago. The narrow trail was made by careful placement of desert stones positioned on the ground, one after another, in two parallel lines leading from nowhere to nowhere. I find strolling this old forgotten path conducive to many empty thoughts, which are a satisfying suggestion of the empty offerings you may be lucky enough to find during your desert hike. At times, I have been tempted to call the outline of these stones *The Path of Wildness.*

If you overnight at Siberia, then be prepared for strong wind, cold air, brilliant stars, and the frequent low rumble and groan of long trains passing nearby. Most will be slow-moving freight trains, numbering dozens of cars, with three to five growling locomotives at the head, and maybe one or two locomotives pushing from the rear, and possibly another squeezed in somewhere in the middle. At least once in the night you may glimpse a fast-moving Amtrak passenger train speed by with brilliant lights flooding the night from every domestic compartment; always moving fast, always west to east. The sight of this civilized, peopled, conveyance is a bit surreal in this lonesome and otherwise dead-of-humanity place, like the passing of a bright, lively mortal through the dull and gray land of the dead. Each and every train which passes will sound its horn four times as they approach the crossing where the dirt road goes over the tracks, and where crossing bells and lights announce the approaching train to the empty, indifferent desert. Each train will issue four horn blasts, three long and one short: blaaaaaaare, blaaaaaaare, blare, blaaaaaaare. A similar blast of four will be heard as the train passes far off past Klondike to the west, and again where the railroad and highway go by Dishbowl Crater to the east. Very few cars will pass on Route 66 during the day or the night. If you are very lucky, and visit between the months of July and September, then you'll likely witness, at night, the flash of lightening upon distant peaks to the south and northeast; though it's unlikely that you'll hear the sound of thunder, the distance being too great, or that any rain will fall where you are, Siberia being one of the driest places anywhere on earth.

Do not be surprised if you sense something watching you in the night. Desert foxes emerge from their den at sundown to hunt in the dark, and their natural curiosity may lead them to pause and watch you from some distance out. If you are very lucky you might catch sight of their eyes gazing at you from the dark, reflecting the light of your flashlight. How suspect, strange, and alien we must seem to them. Do they wonder at our motives? Ask themselves why we are here? If only you could reassure the fox that you've no intent to leave or take anything besides your own complacent certitude and weak dependence.

Tongues of rock

Beginning in Siberia, you will want to start your hike early in the morning by heading out towards the northeast. If you must, then use a compass. If you can, then consider the art of dead reckoning. Though, if you are not possessed of a good sense of direction then please do not try this, as the desert here is no place to become lost. Just remember that if you are ever in a pinch and cannot remember your way out, then simply head south and you will eventually run into the railroad, and then the highway. Another simple solution to escape this particular region of desert is to simply follow the apparent course which water might take. Since all rivers in this immediate area drain to an enormous dry lake basin to the southeast, you will eventually arrive at the railroad if you simply pretend to be water, and flow with the watercourse down.

Setting out from Siberia you will immediately come to the railroad tracks. I do not recommend crossing, or even approaching these, which is a sure way to get in trouble should the railroad police catch you, or worse, a train. Instead, I recommend hiking a quarter mile east to cross under the tracks, where a low bridge goes over a flash-flood channel. But watch out for snakes under the bridge, which is a perfect hiding place for such species. After the tracks, you will immediately see a large earthen berm stretching out to the left and to the right. This berm was formed by the railroad using bulldozers in an effort to protect the tracks from flash floods. Coming out from under the tracks, the berm spreads away in long angles out into the desert. Beyond this berm is open desert. When you step past the berm you have now left civilization. Moving away from the tracks you'll probably see some railroad debris such as old steel tracks and wooden ties resting along the edge of the wash, as well as older items such as rusted cans and broken glass—though after the berm you'll only rarely spot anything made by humans, beside periodic Mylar balloons which float out here from birthdays and surprise parties in Los Angeles, to become tangled and entwined in the limbs of creosote and burro bush. Please consider collecting these intruders to take them out of the desert with you when you go. As they no more belong here than you.

From where you are now, look towards the northeast, and you should see a large and ominous Black Mountain standing alone like a dead sentinel. This mountain is your destination. It is about two and a half miles away as the crow flies and will serve as a reliable beacon for the next hour or so of hiking. There is another, still larger, black mountain (volcano, really) directly east of you, but this is not your destination, as it won't lead you far enough from civilization and safety to do any real good. The indifference there being simply too faint to perceive.

When you pass beyond the railroad berm, you will be stepping onto what is simply the most current page of a long geologic story. The hard-packed sandy soil beneath your feet extends downward to depths of dozens or hundreds of feet before reaching bedrock. Further south from this spot the depth of sand grows steadily deeper by hundreds and thousands of feet to a maximal depth of over ten-thousand feet of accumulated alluvium. You are standing then upon an ocean of eroded sediment deposited here over millions of years. That is because the desert around Siberia is the outer edge of what was once a vast valley between the hills and low mountains of the Bristol range to the north, and the much larger Bullion Mountains to the south. The Bullions are those large peaks you can see when you look south from Siberia, and where you may spot one or two red light beacons flashing at night from the highest peaks. Those mountains are very far away. Long ago, the mountains on both sides of the valley were much larger than they are today, and the space between them vast and deep. However, that ancient valley has since been filled in over a long expanse of time by the steady and gradual erosion of the mountains on either side. If we could snap our fingers and suddenly make all the sand which fills the valley disappear, then you would find yourself wishing you had a parachute as you begin falling towards the valley floor far below. Imagine all the time required to fill this enormous empty space with sand. Imagine all wind and rain necessary to complete the feat of eroding, transporting, and depositing all of the loose rock bits which comprise the desert sediment. This fact is still more startling when you consider that much of this sand arrived gradually, via intermittent flash floods which, just once or twice a year, pour from the mountains to add another layer to this long story of sand.

The ground where you now stand is composed of a mixture of many types of rock: from beach-like sand grains, to pebbles, to stones and even very large boulders. All of which were laid down by perennial streams and rivers during wet epochs such as the Pleistocene, or by intermittent flash floods during the current dry desert climate. Try and imagine the countless successive late summer floods which spilled from these mountains out onto the open plains, emerging from narrow and winding canyons onto broad slopes of sand; waters mixed and churning with mud, rocks, boulders, sticks, logs as well as dead plants and animals. Upon exiting the mountain canyons, these fast-moving floods would spread into myriad braided channels, which then diverge, meet and separate again over the course of many miles before at last depositing their load and sinking into the landlocked desert basin or evaporating into the dry, stale air. These violent flash floods are infrequent and intermittent—rarely re-visiting the same open desert course twice in years or decades, as new sediment deposits tend to push subsequent floods to either side of the last course. This is the process which, over many hundreds and thousands of years, did produce the alluvial fans and bajada upon which you now stand, which are made more clearly visible due to the lack of any trees or extensive ground cover.

The desert near Siberia consists of volcanic rock and sand of dark and light coloration. I refer to the darker material as "Tongues of Rock" due to the way these formations stretch across the land for miles north to south. Both the light and the dark rocks are volcanic in origin, having come to the surface of the Earth at different times, to flow and cool after exposure to the atmosphere. The dark-colored rock appears to be from an earlier eruption, consisting of magma, rich in iron, which oxidized as it flowed over the surface of the Earth before at last solidifying into miles-long petrified flows. This is what gives these landforms their "Tongue of Rock" appearance when viewed from high altitude or satellite imagery. The red color of these rocks is due to oxidation after exposure to the Earth's atmosphere. The lighter-colored rocks and sand here appear to be from a different volcanic event, in which the rocks solidified underground, providing little or no opportunity for oxidation. This is the reason for the lighter color of these rocks. Walking across this landscape is as pleasant an experience as reading a book of ancient geologic history, as every mile reveals a new and interesting chapter in the story of the Earth. Keep your eyes open here for bits of petrified wood, as this area did also once host a conifer forest which was apparently killed and covered by the ash of a nearby volcanic eruption; possibly from one of the volcanoes you will see during your journey today.

I hope that you will enjoy your long trek across the open desert from the railroad to the Tongues of Rock, and the experience of investigating the story of the dark and light-colored sands. To maintain your bearings and heading, just keep your eyes on the dark Black Mountain which is your current destination. But again, be careful to not confuse the mountain you are now after with the large black volcanic cinder cone which can be seen further out and to the southeast. If you find yourself running roughly parallel to the railroad while steering towards this more distant dark-colored mountain, then you are probably hiking towards the wrong peak. The mountain you want is the smaller one more to the north, which stands alone and looks something like a black, bell-shaped dome, and for which walking towards will gradually conduct you further and further from the railroad. But beware, for you will soon lose sight of this guide...

Black Mountain begins to disappear while walking on the Tongues of Rock due to the fact that the landscape has begun rising more steeply ahead of you. If you are not good at dead reckoning, then it might be a good idea to bring a GPS unit or compass and maybe a proper map, as this is not a good place to get lost or turned around in, and it is worthwhile to come with proper navigation equipment and skills if you believe you'll need them. I am pretty good at just finding my way in and back, and so when I lose sight of the Black Mountain, I just continue walking uphill in the same direction I was headed. Eventually, if you keep to the same course, then the landscape will begin to level off, and you will again spot Black Mountain, though this peak is now much larger and closer than when you first lost sight of it. At this point, look for stones on the ground displaying the impressive geologic phenomena called desert varnish.

The rocks near the summit of the Tongues of Rock are quite interesting, with many surface rocks resting on the ground in intriguing natural tableau, almost as though they had been positioned here by the landscape designer at a Japanese Zen temple. If you look closely at many of these stones, you will note that they are covered with a deep and rich patina. This dark coloration is quite evident when you pick up one of the stones and examine its underside, which is likely much lighter in color than the surfaces which are exposed to the open air. This phenomenon is called "desert patina" or "desert varnish" and there are several explanations for its origin. Keep your eyes also open for hematite, which is a high-quality form of iron ore. The specimens of hematite here are particularly nice, and may be easily mistaken for meteorite, especially since both rock types are strongly attracted to magnets.

One explanation for desert varnish is the gradual accumulation of impurities which are deposited on the rocks from rainwater. Another idea is that bacteria are the source of the varnish, leaving the dark stains as a waste by-product of their metabolism. In either case, the varnish appears to develop on the rocks at a known rate, which is helpful to researchers who can use this information to date how long a stone has been exposed in the open by noting the relative accumulation of varnish. Another useful function of this knowledge is in determining how long-ago human rock art was inscribed on desert stones, where such marks were made by scraping away the dark varnish. This is done, again, by measuring the amount of desert varnish which has accumulated on the stones since the scraping was first made. The stones which you will find resting so nicely upon the summit of the Tongues of Rock are some of the best examples I've seen of desert varnish, and I highly recommend you take a break from your trek to examine the rocks here. Just please be careful to replace these as you found them for the sake of future passerby to enjoy.

When you can see the Black Mountain again, you are now very near a major landmark on this hike. At the end of the tongues of rock, you will suddenly come upon a small bluff overlooking a large sandy arroyo called Siberia Wash (real name). The wash is always dry, save for the times when sudden and violent flash floods come through. You'll be safe crossing, though definitely check the weather before your hike, as a forecast of rain should keep you on the alert for the sudden, upstream appearance in the wash of a churning wall of water, led by a loudly grinding head of boulders, stones and plant debris. Though the chances of encountering a flash flood are slight, the risk is real, and the likelihood of death should you become caught up in the flood are quite high. As an added precaution, please remember to never set up camp in a sandy wash basin, as this is just asking for trouble. Keep in mind that one of the leading causes of accidental death in the American desert is drowning due to setting up camp in the soft sands of a flash flood arroyo. Desert floods can appear suddenly, and without warning under a cloudless sky due to localized cloudbursts occurring far out of sight higher in the mountains.

From the bluff overlooking Siberia Wash, you can now easily see Black Mountain directly ahead. If you look a bit to the right you'll see a smaller peak with something at the top which I call "The Watcher" due to the fact that it looks like a human figure standing on the top of the hill looking back at you. This Watcher will follow your movements from now until you pass beyond the northwest edge of Black Mountain. Before you move down off the bluff, and into the sandy wash, you'll want to see if you can spot another small wash leading up and out of the larger wash on the other side of the arroyo. This is a good landmark and destination if you want to discover the jeep tracks which are the next section of this guide. It is alright if you don't find the small wash though, as your overall destination is still the Black Mountain which you can likely easily see from where you are.

Descend carefully down the side of the bluff and into the sandy wash. Be careful here as the descent is deceptively dangerous, with loose and slippery footing and many narrow slots and crevasses where you could easily catch a foot and twist an ankle.

Old jeep tracks

"The imaginations excited by the view of an unknown and untraveled wilderness are not such as arise in the artificial solitude of parks and gardens, a flattering notion of self-sufficiency, a placid indulgence of voluntary delusions, a secure expansion of the fancy, or a cool concentration of the mental

106

powers. The phantoms which haunt a desert are want, and misery, and danger; the evils of dereliction rush upon the thoughts; man is made unwillingly acquainted with his own weakness, and meditation shews him only how little he can sustain, and how little he can perform."

-Dr. Johnson

After you cross the Siberia Wash, you will encounter a short, yet steep, climb up and onto the tongue of rock on the far side. As before, watch out, as the crumbly rock surface could cause a bad slip and fall. Once you are up on top, you will find it easy going along the flat surface which inclines very gradually upward in the direction of Black Mountain. This area is curious for its exceptionally flat and even surface, and if you look closely, you might spot some old jeep tracks running in the same direction you are walking. I imagine these tracks were laid down many decades ago by miners, though they remain quite distinct for the fact that there is little rain to wear the marks away, and though the wind is strong and nearly constant here, it is rarely powerful enough to move the small stones which form the outline of the jeep tracks. Keep a lookout here for fine examples of a phenomena called "desert pavement" which is the delicate and seemingly deliberate arrangement of tiny pebbles into a mosaic of stones upon the flat surface of the desert. The process which produces this pavement requires many years of wind, rain, and gravity to bring the stones into just the right place to fit together like a jigsaw puzzle. Call it a miracle if you like, though I see no more wonder here than chance and the mindless will of nature.

Keep the Black Mountain directly ahead of you now, and just a little to your right as you proceed, and you will soon encounter a second wash smaller than the first. From the edge of the tongue of rock you will want to carefully survey the Black

Mountain which is now just across the wash. You will find several small ridges coming off the side of the mountain. There is a ridge at the near edge with a small canyon on either side. Make your way up and into the north-side branch.

Windy Ridge

"There was there felt the force of a presence not bound to be kind to man."

-Henry David Thoreau

About halfway up the small canyon, turn right, and begin climbing carefully up the side towards the ridge above. About halfway up the side, stop...and look around. If you are lucky (and in the right place) you might make out the very faint outline of an animal trail where it crosses the hillside. I discovered this animal trail through the study of satellite imagery, and it was curiosity about the trail which first led me here. Go to the trail, and then follow it towards Black Mountain until you reach the looming flank of that ominous peak. Now that you have reached the mountain look up. Impressive, huh? When I reached this same point, I quickly gave up any idea of climbing Black Mountain. There was simply something about the steepness of the sides, the fact that I was alone, the strong wind, the startling sunlight, and the poor condition of my body—which was already protesting the hike with fatigue and the whispered voice of caution—which together suggested I was done with this upward advance. At least for today. For the record, I have since returned and climbed Black Mountain.

Climb now along the very edge of Black Mountain where it meets the little canyon, and up to the ridge which extends out from the side of the mountain. Walk out on the ridge and find a nice spot for a sit, to look back in the direction of Siberia. Black Mountain is now looming directly behind you. Small canyons falling away on your either side. Looking left you can see "The Watcher" upon his distant perch, watching you still. To the right, the second wash you crossed disappears soon around a bend and into the badlands to the north, to the place you are headed next. In there can be found the Sandman's Bed. If you are lucky the wind is now blowing, blowing hard perhaps. Looking far, directly ahead you can see miles to Siberia and many miles more to the distant Bullion Mountains beyond. So far. So impossibly far.

This is the point when the fear first struck me on this hike. A real anxiety rising from the immensity of the vista before me. The solitude. The uncaring wind. My own growing sense of my body's failing functions and frail durability. How easy it would be to stumble and twist a leg on descent from this place. Somewhere where nobody knows where I am. Someplace I'd not likely ever be found. Sure, someone could find my motorcycle back at Siberia. But what could lead them here to me across such trackless desert, with so many other places to look? Yes. Here I am so clearly vulnerable, and weak, and getting old, and so plainly mortal. The indifference becomes apparent at this point. Especially when I look over my right shoulder at the badlands to the north. Towards the Sandman's Bed, which is my next destination. Again, for the record, the first time I came here I did not have a GPS rescue device, and no one knew where I was. I was truly, utterly, alone and beyond help. Though I hesitate to say so, this factor may be important to the quality of the experience which I am attempting to relate. Though if anyone asks, you did not hear that from me.

The Sandman's Bed

*"Generally speaking, a howling wilderness does not howl: it is
the imagination of the traveler that does the howling."*

-Henry David Thoreau

Look behind you from Windy Ridge. If you came here alone,
could you climb to the top of that Black Mountain at your
back? This challenge proved too much for me, and I found
myself dismissing the thought outright, with vehemence, with
such conviction in fact that I was startled by my own
willingness—eagerness almost—to give up. How could this be?
As climbing Black Mountain was the very reason I had come
here. Now all I could think to do was retreat. And I could not
escape fast enough... If your resolve is greater than mine, then
climb Black Mountain, and hazard a glimpse of deeper
Indifference than my courage or resolve could then muster.
When you are done—or if, like me, you give up—then make
your way carefully back down the side of Windy Ridge the way
you arrived. Though do not go back along the animal trail, and
instead simply go directly to the bottom of the little canyon,
and then up the other side. Below you now, are the badlands.
Make your way carefully down, and then skirt east along the
northern base of Black Mountain until you can see a third
black volcano in the far distance to the east. Turn now to the
north and move straight into the badlands. Note how the wind
suddenly stops here. Where did this vacuum silence come
from? And suddenly the fear is gone, or nearly gone. Maybe it
will soon be replaced by something else?

Wander a bit to the north into the hard and irregular
landscape here. Attempt to get lost a little, and perhaps forget
the reason you came. Within a few minutes the land will dip
down and to the left at what is the start of a small drainage. Go

down into the drainage and follow it as the water would flow, back in the direction of Siberia. You have just passed the furthest point of this journey and will now be making a roundabout return to Siberia, following a new route back in the worthy tradition of Thoreau.

The little watercourse you are on will grow slightly larger with each step. When I came this way, the anxiety I felt up there on Windy Ridge had vanished by this point; and was replaced instead with a confidence which grew in proportion to the erosion of the landscape where I now walked. I believe that the cause of this change was the cessation of the wind, which blew hard up on the ridge, unsettling my nerves with a reminder of these fierce natural circumstances, and the implicit threat of such solitude, and disconnect from the comforting fellowship of my own species. The quiet now of this meandering dry gully hushed my nerves, but perhaps only as much as any illusion of security the mind can invent in dangerous places and compromised circumstance.

Soon your little course will merge into a larger gully, with steeper sides and a sandy bottom. How much water and rain were required to make this sand from solid volcanic rock and granite? Was this done during this current epoch of desert? Or perhaps during an earlier period of geologic time, when the landscape was not desert, and rain fell and flowed here sufficient to produce a perennial stream, with fish, and insects, and birds, brush, trees and an entire green ecosystem? Was this small stream basin carved then from stone by the constant attention of a bursting biome of animate purpose and action? Am I seeing this now in the absence of such seeming purposeful force? Is this thing, which is lacking, in fact the cause of the indifference I sense all around me? The vacuum absence at the cessation of activity? Is this why I can only best comprehend such indifference in the desert? And only after I

111

have wandered far from somewhere, into a nowhere, where memory remains visible only upon the face of stones, and the piles and swirls of sand. My steps begin to slow and falter here. The Sandman's spell begins with comfort and deep wonder. I must not let myself sleep. There's time enough for that after.

After a short distance, the larger gully will widen and then turn gently to the right. Black Mountain is now near at hand, directly to the southeast. It blocks and protects us from discovery. To the east, west and north there is only vast waste and empty. This place is nearly as good as you could hope to find for quiet introspection, though you may need to bring such peace with you. I recommend stopping somewhere here in the sand. Take off your pack. Lay it aside. Sit down on the sand. Pull off your shoes. Then your socks. Lay these aside to dry a bit in the still, sunny air. Take off your shirt. Lay down on the soft sand. Close your eyes now with your head facing upstream, and your feet towards the somewhere where you are headed. Your feet should always face in the direction of your somewhere.

Close your eyes and let the sun blaze. Warmth rises now on your exposed limbs. Feel your skin beginning to heat. Does the sand feel good under your back, bottom, and legs? It should be soft and surprisingly comfortable. Let your mind wander. Note how it does not wander far. There's anxiety again now as you lay exposed and vulnerable in the wilderness. What danger might come of this? What animal could be watching you now from above the gully? What might come padding or slithering up or down the wash towards us? What small things might now be creeping across the sand in our direction? Did I stay too long out here? Do I have enough water to make it back to Siberia safely? Can I remember the way? I am already on a path which is not the one I used to get here? Do I have enough time to make it back? Will I die today, or tonight, out here in the desert? Have I already made some fatal mistake?

Note how these thoughts are different from those on Windy Ridge. Was your thinking so practical on the ridge? Looking out at the impossible landscape, feeling, and hearing the wind, tracing your mortality across some past few decades of your life to this moment? Asking yourself how much more to come, and what if anything, might follow? These were the impressions on the ridge. Not fear, but frightful awe, and an awesome comprehension of irrelevance to the lack of any comprehensible meaning, intent, or purpose in the greater scheme of nature. This is the difference between the naked and raw exposure to indifference, and the mere fear of being alone someplace far and alien.

When you have had your rest at The Sandman's Bed, put your shirt and shoes back on, hoist your pack and continue walking downstream until you spill out into a larger wash. Turn right and go up this wash a short distance—maybe a quarter mile—before turning sharply to the left and heading up and over the ridge. Now you cross the badlands. You might cross here through another couple of washes as you move steadily west. Now's the time to get lost and lose your way to the next stop in our journey. If you do get lost, then do not panic. Just head downstream with the next dry wash you encounter or go back to the last wash. Following any wash or watercourse now towards the south will eventually take you out into the open desert, where you should be able to regain your orientation. And even if you do not, if you continue south now you will certainly eventually encounter the railroad and route 66. But again, do not come here or follow this course unless you can accept the chance that you might make a mistake and find yourself truly lost, with night arriving soon, little water left, and absolutely no idea where to go. This risk is one of the reasons to come.

Campo #1

At this point in the hike, I have rather left you on your own and am now providing only rough guidance to get you from one place to another. This is both deliberate, and a consequence of the fact that, as I type these words, I cannot really think of a good way to guide you along a route that is largely trackless, and without good landmarks. All I can say is that you need to continue west through the badlands until you again encounter Siberia Wash. But do not let the fact of your larger journey and goal distract you from the worthwhile value of attendance to each step through the badlands. In hindsight, if there is any place, I wish I had lingered more on this hike, it is here. There is not much to be found in this waste, which is precisely its attraction; and the uneven up and down of the landscape, somewhat slippery underfoot, gives good traction to the type of reflection my dead muse so often promotes. In fact, I am a little suspicious that these badlands are where the corpse-like inspiration I call my muse first found me, and then followed me back home.

Stop when you reach the eastern edge of Siberia Wash, and then look across the wash for a dark line of rock stretching low and long against the foot of the hills at the other side. This is a dyke of rhyolite which stands in the midst of the wash, very close to the far edge. There are two additional rhyolite chunks in the wash here, closer islets of stone. Move now towards these rocks, visit each if you can, find the surprise treasure hidden here[6], before continuing towards the larger dyke. When you arrive at the largest and furthest dyke, note the fact of shade here, which is something you cannot easily find in this desert. Use the shade now if you need to, though beware black widow spiders in the crevasses of the porous stone.

Maybe you have already noticed now that you are at the dyke, but there is a wooden structure standing alone just a few dozen yards to the west of the dyke. This is "Campo #1" which is a long-abandoned mining camp. The location of Campo #1 is an outstanding desert camp site on the south end of an island in the wash, protected from the floods, and protected from the winds. It is a good place to overnight. I will leave the rest for you to discover on your own, as there is not much here that isn't worth finding any other way than alone.

Dangerous abandoned mine shaft

When you are finished at Campo #1 head south down Siberia Wash. Do you feel that subtle relief of being homeward bound? Are you tempted, as you walk through the sand, by the sight of deep, long, canyons extending off to your right? Do you see the colors in those hills? Do you want to go there now? I thought the same; though I resisted for a while, which was a good thing, as the first few of those canyons will take you too far out of your way, up and into the place I call Deep-Water. I recommend saving your swim into Deep-Water for another hike. I have been there. That place deserves a fresh start—and more importantly, fresh reconnaissance—and an understanding of the area that comes from first successfully completing The Anxiety Hike.

Do you sing? I do not—though I found the walk along the wash from Campo #1 to the abandoned mine shaft a good place to sing. Just about the time you are starting to get into it you should see a large pile of dirt atop a small embankment to the right. This pile marks the site of a vertical shaft dug straight down into the Earth. Approach carefully, as falling in would be very bad. There is a large wooden beam across the hole. Throw a rock in and wonder at the depth. How deep does the desert really go?

This hike is almost over. At least in terms of what I can tell you. The last part is a bit of a risk, as it consists of a freeform walk into the near edge of *Deep-Water*, and a somewhat challenging push out through *The Edge of Deep-Water*, up and over a landscape which is indeed a bit dangerous, will likely provoke some panic, and may lead you to become truly lost if you are not careful. Perhaps it is better you skip The Edge of Deep-Water and just continue down the Siberia Wash towards the railroad. You will find your way back. It is the smart thing to do.

The Edge of Deep-Water

"It is after we get home that we really go over the mountain, if ever."

-Henry David Thoreau

As I write these words, I feel like I am being overly melodramatic at this point in the story. However, I have been to The Edge of Deep-Water three times, and every time I felt the same. It is a scary place, largely due to the fact of exposure, and heat, and distance, and the strange sense that time is running out. It's not like the Indifference I sensed on Windy Ridge, or the unseen threat I pondered at the Sandman's Bed. There is something more real about what I feel every time I go to The Edge of Deep-Water. A sense that the clock is ticking, perhaps a bit too fast. A mild panic that rises as I begin to race back to safety. A sense that the Desert Killer is on its way.

116

From the abandoned mine shaft, continue past the hole and into the small canyon which cuts into the place I call Deep-Water. Walk and walk. To the left, and then the right, as the canyon twists and turns. Admire the color in the walls. Admire the plants. After a bit, things will open up to the right, revealing a very interesting and different type of badlands, consisting of rolling hills and deeply faulted canyons. On your extreme right side, a small mountain rises to a high point. About halfway up there is an "Old Miner" squatting and watching, taking over your surveillance where The Watcher of Siberia Wash left off. This is where you will discover *The Home of Faith*. Look to the north now. Look hard. No faith is needed.

Some distance further, you will need to make a sharp left and then strike for the low, and very near, hills to the south. Though the climb is not too difficult, I do think it is dangerous. The ground here consists of crumbly, slippery granite and very narrow channels and crevices where feet could easily slip, get caught, or meet a rattlesnake. Take care now. Make your way safely to the top.

When you arrive at the summit you have reached The Edge of Deep-Water, from which you have also just emerged. Though in fact, your encounter with the Deep-Water Wilderness was only passing, and fleeting. Turn now and look back. Take in that view. Don't you want to go deeper? Take off your pack and sit down for a bit. Let the wind press from behind. Look over your shoulder towards Siberia. You are almost safe again. All you need to do is make it down through the hills, out over the tongues of rock, onto the alluvium, and out across the open.

"Come home, and expect such welcome as is due to him, whom a wise and noble curiosity has led, where perhaps no native of this country ever was before."

-Dr. Johnson

Still there?

I'm glad you've come with me
So far

From this point,
Things may get a little strange
For what follows,
Is my own report from the wild:

First,
I'll tell you about what I discovered,
In the wildness of Japan

Second,
I'll relate what I found,
In the wildness of the desert

Both accounts are real

I hope you'll stick with me,
A little further
I promise you *nothing* in return

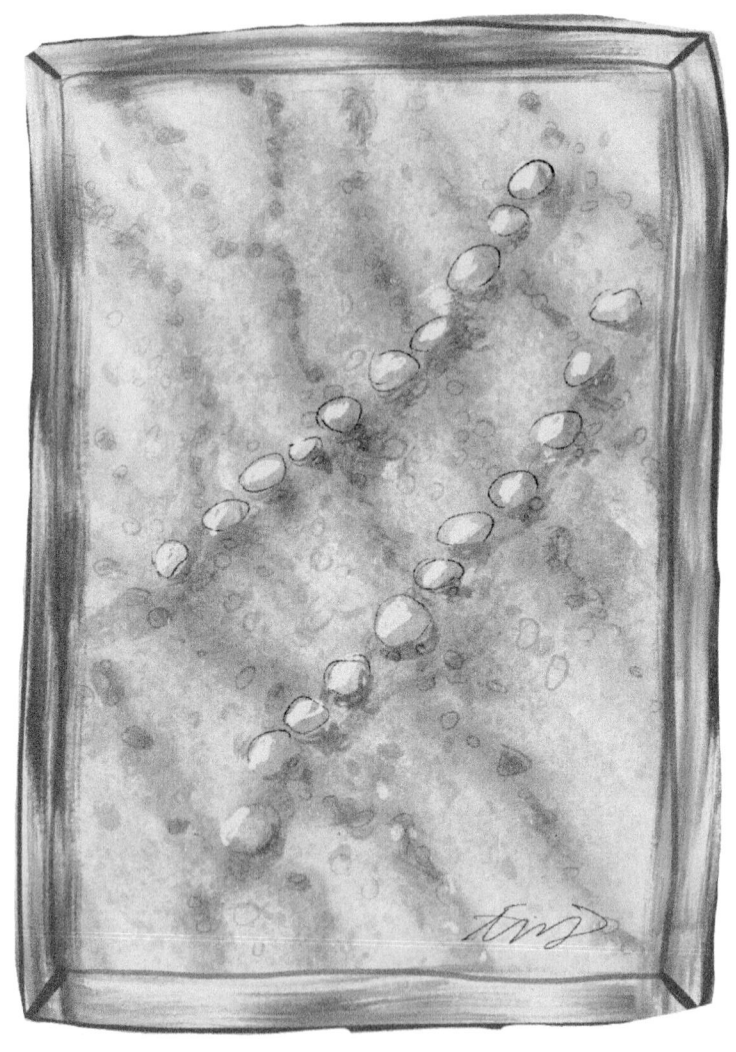

The Path of Wildness

THE PATH OF WILDNESS

Mustering the courage to live

*"Persons who have wandered, or been
expelled, out of the common track of
things, even were it for a better system,
desire nothing so much as to be led back.
They shiver in their loneliness, be it on
a mountaintop or in a dungeon."*

-Nathaniel Hawthorne

This chapter was originally composed in Japan, and before I
began going alone in earnest. I wrote *The Path of Wildness* in
response to the many young people who contacted me during
my time as a Japan-based YouTube content creator. Young
people dreaming of Japan, yet unable to muster the courage or
resources to make their dream real and writing to ask me how
this trick was done, and what advice I could offer to help them
get away from whatever unsatisfactory life they were living. I
responded with *The Path of Wildness*, which is a metaphor for
courage and action, and a reminder of the risk of waiting too
long, and a challenge and method for getting unstuck.

The Path of Wildness

As I near fifty, I am becoming increasingly aware that my situation is like a man holding his breath in a sealed container of water, with less than a minute of consciousness remaining. Now is the time to scratch something meaningful on the wall to share what I have seen and learned:

> *The Path of Wildness is easy to find*
> *The course of a stream*
> *Leaves blown in the wind*
> *A beast's track through the brush*
> *And the direction of our first inclination*

The Path of Wildness is an answer and response to a prescribed way of life which may leave some individuals with a sense that their living is little more than a series of pre-determined, step-like episodes between birth and death. The stages of living between these events: childhood, adolescence, adulthood, parenthood and senior, are themselves natural, and in accord with the needs of the species, and most individuals. Many find satisfaction in living this course, and to these individuals I have little to say. Others though, long for something more, something innate, genetic, and seemingly calling. Adventure and change can give a degree of satisfaction and relief, yet even these may seem too tame, and the results often only temporary. To those who feel drawn to something beyond the entertainment and stimulation of senses, I offer a walk along *The Path of Wildness*. Don't bother penciling the event into your schedule, preparing a pack with goodies and supplies, or even inviting a friend along, for this experience is along the course of your first inclination, and you must surely always go alone.

The problem: life has no apparent meaning

My adventure videos on YouTube have produced a steady stream of email from people who tell me about the dreams they cannot quite bring themselves to live, and their fear of being alone, and feeling their lives do not matter. However, nobody ever says it that way, and instead they cloak these worries as simple life anxieties or blame their trepidation and inaction on various personal or familial infirmities and challenges. They do this to convince themselves these simple facts are the true cause of their churning worry and hesitation. They attempt to avoid a deeper fear. A hidden threat which is more real and threatening to a quality life than any surface level anxiety. It is a demon of sorts, lurking in the shadows of conscious thought, peeking with knowing eyes in the direction of our mortality, pointing a crooked finger at the hazy terminal point of our life, while offering a suggestive grin that nothing will be found beyond. This thought, along with the weighty implication it bears that life is without intrinsic meaning, appears to be the more real and tactile cause of the concern I sometimes read in the words of those who write to me. I never point this out though, as I suspect they prefer I go along with their bluff, and humor them with a response in keeping with their stated concern. Reality, after all, can be a fearful thing to face. However, I will now attempt a more honest answer, reflective of my own life experience, and sincere interactions with others.

This light and living we now know offers a stark contrast to the nothingness we intuitively sense existed before our birth, and the same nothingness we fear a return to after life is done. In fact, this fear is far worse than a return to nothingness, as we are each capable of holding a vision of Hell in our minds more terrible and real than the worst damnation preached from any austere and authoritative pulpit. This greater terror is our sense

124

that the universe can get along without us, that our life and living are of little real consequence in any way, and that our best efforts will account for little beyond the temporary comfort given to the handful of individuals we share and interact with, before death takes us away utterly, permanently, and forever. This is the real terror so many struggle to avoid, which reason and honest inquiry coldly suggest as true. An abject fear of ultimate insignificance and meaninglessness in the face of the curious fact of temporary life in an otherwise lifeless universe.

I do not understand why the thought of death—real death, absolute death, with no chance of recovery, salvation, or continuation—is more tolerable to some than others. However, I suspect this acceptance may relate to some level of comfort and familiarity with being alone. Not that anyone will be alone after death, as even the concept of alone then would be wishful thinking. Nevertheless, during life, if we can abide our own company for extended periods of time, then the thought of being without others, or ourselves even, after death, may somehow become more palpable and acceptable; a more familiar, intangible something, and somewhere, less feared, as accepted, or perhaps resigned to. To such a person, a life without absolute meaning may be acceptable: days, months, and years of striving to no absolute end alright, and nothing to fear. To such an individual, the journey itself becomes its own purpose, the momentary satisfaction and good feelings connected with virtue their own worthy end, where virtue is defined simply as the pursuit of objective well-being for ourselves and others. Death then offers no transition, but is seen as a simple, final, stop. A period, and ending of effort, and of striving, and of reflection towards understanding which yields nothing more than transitory and ultimately meaningless gain to ourselves and those to follow. But is this a bad thing? If yes, then it's understandable that many protest, recoil, and fly from such thoughts. But if no, then our breathing can relax as we measure each inhalation as one of the few we get; and use the fuel of this living to move our body and activate our brain in such a way as to create our own meaning in these passing moments, and to pursue objective goodness in the willful expression of perceived best ends.

So, what words can I say to those who write to me asking my thoughts regarding their worldly dilemmas? When my suspicion tells me their real concern is actually a fear of their own unimportance, and the utter finality of death? In most cases I will engage their most direct questions, and give the best answer and suggestion I can, given my untrained, and un-credentialed qualifications. I wish though, that I could speak to them more plainly, and tell them that their deeper fears are real, and then ask them to explain their terror for my own benefit, and then hear my claims which I hope may benefit them. Perhaps then we could both gain from a more honest and humane inquiry and inquisition into facts than any civilized, restrained, or judicial discourse could provide. For my part I am now prepared to lay my humble case before any who may care to hear.

Opportunity; available light

Mind is an instantiation of consciousness, formed of energy organized within the brain along pathways designed of genetics, and molded through the unique living of each individual. There is no soul in the sense of anything transcendental or eternal. The fact that our materials and energy are everlasting—having been used by others before us and destined for reuse by the yet unborn—is testament to the fact that our person is temporary and ephemeral. We are, individually and collectively, a brief, dim and fast fading spark and flash of material and energy in the darkening night of the universe. In this fact we discover both our dilemma and great potential: the

126

challenge being to remain upright in the face of our utter, fleeting insignificance, while engaging whatever meek will we can muster towards observation, reflection, and art, while the light and sound of the universe wash across our senses.

Without apparent purpose, we are left to decide for ourselves whatever meaning, or significance should guide our days and actions. This is the great dilemma of the individual, which demands forthright acceptance of the facts of the observable universe; and withholds any complete explanation or guidance. You must stand alone. You must recognize your solitude. You must hold yourself upright despite unstable footing and the approach of death. You must withstand the awful winds growing stronger; and control your trembling hands while strange howling emanates from the wilder places, and no trail or trodden path indicates the direction of safety. From here—if you can quiet the heart and gain control of your senses, overcome, or learn to tolerate feelings of isolation, loneliness, and fear—then you will be prepared to make your own one-way path through the wild, to step where the weeds are tangled, and small, biting creatures lurk with hairy legs, slicing jaws and venomous sting. This is your path to follow. A truly dangerous and terrifying route none has ever trod or may ever again follow. The light is faint now, and growing fainter as the evening and night of your days grows near. Follow the dusk and note the sights. Speak of what you see. Describe your world in writing, or painting, or photography, or spoken word. Poetry especially, is a natural and well-suited vehicle to capture this ever-declining experience. Walk your path and observe, and then tell the story of your own brief available light.

Health: exercise and eating well

"Wisdom is an organized life."

-Immanuel Kant

Your good philosophy depends upon your body, which relies upon your health, which rests upon the choices you make as to exercise and what you eat and drink. Devote some time early in life to an understanding of what makes good bodies, and then take care of yourself accordingly. What follows is a summary of my own, imperfect exercise and diet solutions.

I exercise daily. However, my exercise routine is light, easy and requires little time. My base workout is a fifteen-minute pool swim. My swimming style is very low impact. I do a gentle breaststroke for five laps, and another five laps backwards breaststroke, alternating these two styles between each lap. The backwards breaststroke is something a swim instructor taught me; and involves simply resting face up on the water (like you would do with a conventional backstroke) though instead of reaching back over your head to do a reverse crawl, simply lift your arms to your sides (while keeping your arms in the water) before then stretching out your arms to give a nice stroke until your hands are again at your waist, and your arms parallel to your body. This stroke takes a little practice, but when you have got it down the process is easy. This swim is low impact and very relaxing, as you can look up at the sky while gliding gently through the water. I especially enjoy this swim in the evening at sundown, when I can watch the first stars twinkle into view as the azure Southern California sky fades to black. When enjoying this backwards breaststroke, just beware you do not bang your head on the far end of the pool as your mind floats off with the clouds...

As mentioned, my swim is my base exercise, and I do this every day. However, I also enjoy walking to provide a lower body workout. To this end, I typically walk between two and four miles daily, either spread out over several small walks (like a fast mile during my breaks at work), or one very long walk at the start or end of the day. If, for whatever reason, I need to skip some exercise, it will be my walk, as the swims are not optional, and can only be missed for reasons such as illness or lack of access to a pool. Rain or cold weather are no good reasons to not swim.

KURT'S IMPERFECT DIET
But much better than what I was doing before...

- 5:00 AM – Wake up and drink a glass of water
- 5:15 AM – Shave, shower and then "drink" a blended vegetable smoothie made of:
    - Kale
    - Spinach
    - Broccoli
    - Carrot
    - Beet (lots of this)
      Note: I blend four glasses of this mixture ahead of time, which I keep in the fridge. I do not add anything to the smoothie other than the above ingredients and a little water or lemon juice to help get the blending started.
- 5:30 AM – Single, large fried egg with a slice of buttered whole wheat toast which I share with the dog while watching the news on TV.
- 8:00 AM – Large mixed salad (same ingredients used in the smoothie, but with two handfuls of nuts and dried berry trail mix). I sometimes use lemon juice for dressing.
- 11:30 AM – Bowl of homemade chili with a slice of whole-wheat bread. I make a huge vat of chili every other Sunday,

which I then portion out during the weeks to follow. The chili consists simply of a variety of beans and lots of finely chopped veggies. I season with a tablespoon of cumin and another tablespoon of chili powder.

- 3:00 PM – Small bowl of lightly salted popped popcorn as a mid-day snack. I pop a week's worth of popcorn on Sunday nights, which I then store in my cubicle at work. An alternative to the popcorn is a few slices of unsulfured and unsweetened dried mango. Over time, the mango has almost come to replace the popcorn.
- 6:00 PM – Enjoy another smoothie (same as above).
- 8:00 PM – Prepare and enjoy a healthy dinner. I am lucky, as my wife is an excellent cook, and she makes outstanding Japanese meals for our dinner. I eat as much as I like of whatever she makes, which is always good and healthy, and satisfies whatever want of gluttony may linger at the end of the day.

This menu is my own and reflects my limited sensibilities regarding taste. I am sure that someone more adept in the kitchen might find better and more satisfying alternatives. Of key importance here is the absence of processed foods, sugary drinks, or excessive sweets of any sort. I do allow myself an occasional fast-food meal with my family, and an infrequent indulgence in salty snacks such as chips, or sweet desserts like a cookie or a piece of candy. Popcorn at the movies is a must, as well as a few other simple and periodic indulgences which help to give my life spice and interest, without taking away too much from my efforts at eating well. As for drinks, I limit my intake of coffee to no more than two cups a day (three if I am writing), and I try to avoid fruit juice (too much sugar) and sodas. A beer or glass of wine are fine in the evening, though these seem to hold less appeal for me with each passing year. Starbucks is a must! My favorite is a Grande-sized, extra-hot mocha with two pumps of syrup and whipped cream—after all, everyone's gotta have an indulgence or two to punctuate the serious and difficult work of living well. I occasionally enjoy this particular treat in the evening, after work, when I sit down to answer my personal email, as I find the sugar/caffeine boost to be a nice stimulation to my improved human response.

I cannot emphasize enough how important I have found diet to be in the pursuit of a happy, balanced life. I was 47 years old when I developed this diet, and sadly spent so many years feeling tired, anxious, irritable, unproductive, and downright unhappy, before I learned the very common-sense fact that what I ate and drank, and how much I moved, impacted greatly the biochemistry of body and mind. If you choose to attempt only one aspect of my proposals in this book, then I recommend the adoption of a healthy diet and light program of exercise as the thing to do.

Action: The Path of Wildness

Once healthy, and in a position of understanding regarding the possible deeper fear and trial which makes life such a challenge to those who wish to live a meaningful life, as well as peace of mind when thinking of what apparently does not follow when life is through, you may then be ready to act in the direction of wisdom. Indeed, you may be prepared to rise to your full stature as a man or woman of reason, to apply this faculty towards the higher, perhaps seemingly more worthy acts of a well-lived life. This then, is the time to step upon *The Path of Wildness.*

> *The Path of Wildness is easy to find*
> *The course of a stream*
> *Leaves blown in the wind*
> *A beast's track through the brush*
> *And the direction of our first inclination*

131

Do not mistake the concepts of "wilderness" and "wildness," which are related yet distinct terms. *Wilderness* is a place commonly regarded as devoid of most human influence. Stretches of desert in the American West, the far reaches of the Arctic and Antarctic, and most areas of the Earth's oceans are good examples of wilderness. Few such places on Earth remain utterly untouched by humanity, though many are nevertheless quite wild, and capture the spirit and essence of regions where humans are more alien than familiar. *Wildness*, on the other hand, is the landscape of freedom. Wildness is less a place, and more a region of uncertainty, risk, and very real danger. Wildness is a feature of wilderness, though it is entirely possible for a well-trained, outfitted, and prepared human to enter wilderness without venturing very far into wildness. However, those who step into wildness may do so without ever leaving their home; in fact, they may enter wildness from the comfort of their recliner, or in the company of friends and family—though in practice wildness is most easily accessed through wilderness, which is one of the reasons I have spent so much of my life alone in the outdoors.

Why should someone venture into wildness? Why risk the danger, isolation, and fatigue of exploring alone (even among others) where chance or bad choices may leave you crippled or mortally wounded? There are several benefits which vary in degree, depending upon the character and interests of the explorer, though one benefit is of special use to all, as it grants to the user a most useful skill and habit, and which, through training, can transform the timid, fearful, and meek, into brave, spirited explorers. That quality is simply the character of courage in the face of the unknown, and a willingness to step boldly into seemingly dangerous regions of ignorance and uncertainty; to confront our weakness and shortcomings in open field, where neither can hide, and must instead be viewed for what they really are; and once surveyed, then likely dismissed as unworthy intimidators, whom we order to stand aside as we stride past into the deeper darkness and cold. Not pride, nor unwholesome confidence, shall replace these fears, as these too cannot fail to fall away during our struggle through the wild places. Indeed, most superfluous human traits are vulnerable to being lost along the way, as the close cutting branches, vines and thorns pull away everything which sticks out from our person, and which is not essential to our truer character and inner strength. This is the singular gain and ambition of movement along *The Path of Wildness*. To wear away our excess, refine our better spirit, and help us develop and maintain the courage necessary to live well, as long as the light continues to shine in our eyes.

> *The Path of Wildness is easy to find*
> *The course of a stream*
> *Leaves blown in the wind*
> *A beast's track through the brush*
> *And the direction of our first inclination*

I have described The Path with the above words deliberately in order to leave clues in the commonplace experience of nature which are easy enough to follow, and as a simple training of sorts for the more challenging foray of trust in our personal instinct. I have a reason for relying on instinct, though I understand that instinct is not always right, and in fact may often be quite wrong and dangerous. Nevertheless, despite the risks, instinct is something we all seemingly have, and a sense we can start with when doubt and uncertainty threaten to immobilize our movement. There are times for rest, and times for action, and most of us can easily sense when change is needed; though sometimes we lack the will or conviction to make the first step. It is at times such as this that I recommend moving boldly onto *The Path of Wildness*. This is done by probing our immediate senses for a hint of which way to go,

133

and as long as the urging does not cause us to walk over a cliff in our first step (steps and cliffs are, of course, figurative in many cases) then we should lift our foot and begin moving, or lift our will and push forward with thought, resolve, voice, interaction or whatever form of human living might be involved. We move. We start. We have direction... It may not be the best direction, but courageous movement away from irrational fear or unwarranted timidity is often its own reward, and course correction can usually be made once we are underway.

Once upon *The Path*, the brave explorer should expect two things: danger and treasure. The first is very real and may wound, cripple, or even kill. Expect to emerge from your foray bleeding, lame and perhaps a bit deranged for the experience. Yet, a wholesome perspective might view such damage as nothing more than the expected price of discovering treasure where none like you has ever ventured. New explorers may hope (and likely succeed) in carrying away fresh wealth in the form of possessions, status, or acclaim from the lonely wild lands. These can indeed be had, in abundance in fact, though the glitter and sparkle of such tangible gain may appear as rust to those who go still further in search of the intangible treasures of mind and experience. These brave individuals will most likely return from their ventures exhausted to the point of collapse, pale with blood loss, and slightly mad from the close proximity they achieved to the source of the terrifying howling which can only be heard in the most extreme frontiers of dark and bleak wildness. Their pockets will certainly be torn and empty, and they may be unable to speak clearly of the wonders they have seen, though this is less due to any defect in the speaker's voice, and, more commonly, is a result of the hearer's excess comfort and certainty, which blocks the ears to truth as surely as beeswax. I recommend applauding anyone who returns alone from the wild lands, whether they bear treasure in both arms or gleaming ear to ear within the broad expanse of a blessed, mad smile. Do this, for each is a person of courage, someone who has broken clean of the quicksand of complacency and fear, and who is exercising those most rare and critical faculties of the human species: courage, freedom, and autonomy. But remember also that some who step upon *The Path* will never return. Some will become lost. Others will die. Still more may give up and return by some secret way to rejoin those, who, in fear, remain huddled together in warmth and comfort, and possibly some degree of lifelong despair. These are the things you can expect upon *The Path of Wildness.*

Go then when you feel lost. Step fast, when you suspect your confusion or hesitancy are heeding some unworthy instinct, and are borne of the fear of suffering, and not suffering itself. Move swiftly now in the direction of your first instinct. Call your best critical faculties to the fore, and demand they guide your every footfall. Expect to tire and fall, be ready to suffer, understand that you may die, though know also that along the way, with every step and action, you are living the truest, most noble and worthy venture of your life.

Result: Creating meaning

Those who venture upon *The Path of Wildness* will find a meaning of sorts in the energy, joy, and experience of living a life of courage, a life of periodic misstep, mistake and failure, tempered with breakthrough, discovery and understanding. Taken together, these qualities cause life to acquire a depth and character which is humbling, satisfying, and reassuring. Our living becomes a beautiful sum of many parts: sour, sweet, bitter, raw, and savory. A delicious banquet of days which fills our mind like a feast fills our stomach, and gives us pause along the way, and in the end, to rest in sated comfort at the fullness of our life.

Notes from my muse

I wrote the following verses during an early period of inspiration from my muse, while still living in Japan, and under the influence of the green, lush, watery, and very wild and geologically young mountains of the Japan Southern Alps. The words and phrases here are much simpler than what comes to me now in the desert, conveying less my thoughts about The Great Indifference (which I had not yet recognized in nature) and more simply, my paradoxical understanding that there may be no living after life is done, and that the universe holds no precious mandate for our lives other than to simply stay alive as long as we can, and perhaps to pass our genes into another generation. The words below were originally augmented with images, which you can see at the web address in entry seven of the book's appendix.

No dragons here
only darkness

~

No more purpose
than to outlive ourselves
and then really
not even that

~

I stand alone
in the cold

confused
lost
yet content

~

Avoid excess certainty

~

Erect no edifice
you're not willing
to destroy

~

Biology informs me
I'm corrupt
and degenerate

~

Ignorance is my constant companion
ever at my ear, whispering nothing

~

Fearful musings are best

~

The howling always comes
from further than you are
willing to go

~

I don't fear being wrong
I fear believing I'm right

~

Death is comprehendible
that's why we hide

~

Your own face
is fearful here

~

Every step
a triumph of will

~

Meditate too long
and the way is lost

~

There's no need to venture outside
to explore in wild places
curiosity, reason, instinct, and courage
are the sole necessities of adventure

~

Mt. Wildness is a place
more terrifying than fear
more remote than the unknown
for it is both

~

There are no fresh starts
only new steps

~

There are no bridges here
where streams are cold and fast

~

Mt. Wildness
is the landscape of fear
a truly dangerous place

~

There's a woodsman's cabin
on the near slope of Mt. Wildness
abandoned many years

139

~

*Go alone
and any road
can become a path*

~

*After a certain point
we all begin to dissolve*

~

*The blessing
of becoming lost*

~

*Ordinary light
becomes strange
and stranger still*

~

*Innocence renders the initial step unnecessary;
for youthful movement is from the first intuitive,
earnest and seemingly irrevocable*

~

*Sometimes go
where you do not want to go*

140

~

Mt. Wildness is a dark place
full of light

~

If you fear dark places
then stay where you are
otherwise come
where none can be your guide

~

Let wildness guide
never trust it to lead
lest you never return

~

Move or stop if you are so inclined
have courage for either action

~

The map of indecision

~

Any road
can become the path

~

*Time and distance must always impart change
too long or far and friends become strangers,
longer still foreign and longer yet alien*

~

*The features on your face
trace the course of the path*

~

*Attitude coupled with action
cause the path to appear*

~

*Push into the haze
expecting nothing more
than an opportunity
to become lost*

~

*Faces become strange
too long on the path*

~

*Get busy
before the curtain starts to fall*

142

~

One step and you're on the path

~

Precedence is abhorrent
to those upon the path

~

Those who stare very long at the light
must surely go blind

~

Either course will do

~

The light is not an end

~

Companionship is a warm distraction

~

The path is outside
though not always outdoors

~

Tunnels aren't dark enough
find another way

~

The path runs through the machine

~

Bridges aren't real
find another way

~

A single step is sufficient

~

The way is clearer still
under cover of night

~

Keep walking
the sun is setting after all

~

When I was 18 ideas flashed past my
consciousness too fast and fleeting to
catch or even properly apprehend.
At 28 I squeezed them from my

mind with crayons and loud music;
raw, textured notions wholly adolescent
and shaped like cliché. 38 allowed no
time for such nonsense. 48 finds the
ideas returned though now I'm too
tired and fed up to attempt to lead,
and instead follow meekly wherever
the sunlight moves, seeking warmth
and thoughtful respite in whatever
time remains.

~

Instilling fear and the suspension of
critical thinking are the methods of
those who themselves fear and refuse
to think. Refugees of reason huddled
in the dark, begging company and
offering stale sustenance if only
you'll acquiesce.

~

Stationary strides are longest

~

Only individuals can have courage,
for the group can never truly be brave

~

If you ever doubt your way
and question right or left
choose the darker, dense, and overgrown route

145

for this is where your ignorance is thick
and where passage will surely
come at a price

~

Wildness is found
wherever courage
provokes another step

~

The Path of Wildness is a solution
for those not seeking escape

~

The slant of sunlight and shadow
also mark the way

~

Expect curves upon the path

~

Only life can traverse the path

~

The path of wildness
is a hiking philosophy
and a theory of adventure

~

I'd offer my hand as guide
only then we'd lose our way

~

Shadows lie along the path
shadows point the way
the darker the better

~

The Path of Wildness is purely secular
and in no way spiritual
Biology is the defining and controlling factor
there is no sentience guiding our steps
save perhaps the collective experience
encoded in our genes

~

Thoughts grow feral
on The Path of Wildness
linger long
utterly wild

~

I expect to die here
and soon...

~

I'd like to share with you a great recipe for solitude: simply talk,
act, think or believe unlike others

~

Beware the far side of Mt. Wildness
where our words become babble

~

The only streams here
are cold, fast, and treacherous

~

There's a howling on the mountain
something worthy of fear

~

I fear no social circumstance
for I've been to Mt. Wildness

~

There's a howling
in the darker brush

~

The old shack
at the end of the road

~

*To walk the path
is to adventure on life*

~

*Making life
into an adventure*

~

The frontier of relevance

~

*Any road can become a path
if your step is resolute
and your thoughts quite alone*

~

*You and I are dissolving
day by day*

~

*Dissolution is genetic, bodily and
seemingly essential. do, make and
say what you must before everything
turns to sand.*

149

~

There's a sea below Mt. Wildness
a howling thing roams the woods
and a woodsman's cottage on the near slope

~

I'd rather not
know by instinct
without a thread
of honest reflection

~

Trails are courses

~

What trails do you follow?
what paths do you blaze?

~

Honest virtue
requires no accolade

~

Suppress
or ignore
appetite

150

~

We're all
crippled and suffering

~

Hesitate long
and the path will be gone

~

Practice your art

~

Paths are formed by instinct
trails by consensus

~

I'm making a sign on the frontier of Mt. Wildness
my hope is that it will help keep travelers safe
but not too safe

~

The darkness is repelled by courage
step towards it and it moves away
though one day it will not

~

Return by another way
an unknown way

~

The course of your first inclination
is nothing more
than a catalyst to action

~

They're all dying words
make 'em count

~

Play a bit longer outdoors
before you at last
must go in

~

Abandoned paths
everywhere you look

~

Fast movement
hinders progress

~

Sanction is petty compensation
for a lifetime upon the straight and narrow

~

You are not on the path
if the way is very easy
for very long

~

The most fearful thing
is the distant howling

~

The path is fearful
and dark

~

Failure is tolerable

~

Light your own way
up the slopes of Mt. wildness
where the dawn never comes

153

~

Birds always fly along the path
leaves always blow along the path

~

If you are ever uncertain how to start
simply follow the leaves
and tread in the direction of bird flight

~

Father and son can walk the path
just never together

~

The surest sign you've left the path
is when you meet another along the way

154

The Path of Wildness is easy to find
The course of a stream
Leaves blown in the wind
A beast's track through the brush
And the direction of our first inclination

The Pirate Ride

GOING ALONE

Discovering a universe without apparent meaning

"A major breakthrough of the Scientific Revolution—perhaps its greatest breakthrough—was to refute the intuition that the universe is saturated with purpose."

-Steven Pinker

The Great Indifference is a perspective which yields an improved understanding of the apparent true nature of the universe. It is a place of clear thought, and relentless truth. The way there is never easy, never marked, and can only be reached in solitude, and when the only chance of return is under the power of one's own volition. What you find there may be worth the journey, even if only you alone can understand or appreciate the prize.

There is no road or trail to The Great Indifference, for followers must always lose the way. Strike out at once along the direction of your first inclination, and your own path will soon be discovered. Note what you find, or do not find, as discovery alone is its own satisfaction. And whatever you later relate to others will fall like alien words upon ears plugged and deafened by fraternity, solidarity, and the warm comfort of common society. Only your fellow travelers in wildness might understand, though their own solitary venture may insulate their ears to whatever vain utterances you elect to voice.

I recommend this way to those who are ready to lose, prepared to be wrong, and desirous of truth ahead of comfort, peace, or immortality. Come this way for the sake of virtue, for a sound mind, an even temper, a restful heart, and at last, an honest death; an end without hope of reward, reawakening, or revelation; a fixed point of terminus punctuated upon the tail end of eternity, which is everything after the end of one's living.

The vista of The Great Indifference will direct your gaze to your bruised, sore, and bleeding feet, which are the instruments of your arrival in that august place. The pain will grow intense with your notice. A gratifying reality. How sweet the moment of awakening; when the uncaring, corpse-like gaze of reality makes precious the breath of this moment, and the next, without thought for any breath beyond, which is only a wishful, potential vapor; nor the breaths already consumed, which have dispersed to mingle with the universal atoms, to never again return orbit 'round our fleeting mortal constitution.

I would tell you the way to The Great Indifference if I truly thought I could. Though if you go where I said it was found, then the telling would guarantee its absence. Go instead on your own, by your own motive force, along a way only you can see. Alone, and accepting of your solitude, aware you may never come back; and if you do, that you may never find words to adequately convey what you truly found.

Notes from my muse

When I talk about going alone some may think I'm referring to hiking and camping all by oneself. That's partially right. But mostly I'm referring to a mental endeavor to seek after and develop life principles without the reinforcing comfort of authority, dogma, or consensus. This doesn't require thinking up the ideas oneself, but instead using reason to discern if a

159

proposition is true, and fits with the reality of the world around us. That's going alone. It's only coincidence that being alone in very wild places is an excellent forum for rendering truth from the abundance of comforting propositions and stories we tell one another to keep back the dark. When you're alone in the dark there's nowhere the truth can hide.

~

Emily and I lingered at the beach tonight until it was nearly dark. Just before we left, a middle-aged man arrived limping badly and wearing nothing more than a swimsuit and a beach towel around his neck. He deposited the towel on a rock and limped with difficulty straight into the sea. Once in the cold water—and free of his bad leg—he began swimming powerfully out to sea, diving under a few large waves before making it clear of the surf. We watched him swim straight and direct, further and further, as the night got darker and darker. We saw him swim past a family of dolphin passing far beyond the last rocks, in water more than fifty feet deep. The man never veered his course or turned either up or down the coast, but kept straight for open ocean, swimming hard and fast. He must have been more than a quarter mile out when darkness overtook our efforts to follow. My last sight of the man was a single swing of his arm rising above the now black sea. I noticed the streetlights were on as Emily and I made our way back to the motorcycle— and I wondered if these would guide the man back to shore when he'd had enough of his solo nighttime winter ocean swim.

~

I'm haunted by the desert now. The pull is powerful and relentless. Like a vacuum drawing something to nothing.

At the bookstore just now, I discovered a book titled "Route 66 Ghost Towns." I eagerly read through the sections on the desert railroad communities of Essex, Amboy, Bagdad, Ludlow, Newberry Springs, and Daggett. The chapter ended with no mention of Siberia. It would seem I've made a very good choice in selecting Siberia as my adopted hometown.

~

By this time tomorrow I'll be in Siberia. I'll arrive about an hour before sundown, as temps begin to descend from midday highs around 110 degrees (43 C.). There are no ghosts in Siberia, though there is much that is dead. The void left by humanity passing away here has made room for possession by the wind, the heat and cold, and the steady progress of time. These things ignore my presence, though they'd appear different if I was not alone. I'd see only ruin and desolation with another. I'd see ghosts which were never there.

~

I leave a thinning trail of connection with every mile I put between my life and the desert. This thread grows so slender that 100 miles out I dangle like a spider on a silk strand. The melodramatic abyss looms—a humorous caricature of nature, if only it weren't so real. I hang there for a day, in the wind and the sun, knowing the threat of exposure is nothing compared to the frailty of that one, long, slender thread.

~

The steep and rugged mountains of Japan never scared me. Even that time I ran from the mother boar, and again (several times) when giant hornets swarmed to check me out. The mountains were far too civilized with life to offer any real threat. Not human life, but life itself, the mere fact that the landscape had a pulse, and a vibrant one at that, dissuaded my fear and alleviated my apprehension. Even to die in those remote, unpeopled mountains, would be to pass in the embrace of what is both familiar and alive.

The desert offers no such comfort. What lives there is sparse, mute, and still. There's little hum, or buzz, or grunt. Just some howl from time to time, which carries lonesome sentiment and a desperate pleading. Even birdsong sings of solitude. The wind speaks loudest here. And the sun burns its case without respite, from sunup, to sundown.

I fear the desert. Even before I go.

~

I'm halfway to Siberia and thinking of that long 100-mile thread I mentioned earlier today. Could it be that the thread actually originates out here? How alike the unthinking wastes of nature and the timeless nonexistence before birth and after death.

~

During the night at Siberia, I left camp to wander alone over the desert in search of night things. Nocturnal spiders and snakes, and the things which stare from the dark with glimmering eyes. And the stars which come out, and the moon in its time. The wind too enjoys the night, moving in warm gusts over the land, always inward, towards the deep center of the desert. While thus employed during my nighttime hike, I came upon that stone-lined footpath I've mentioned before. With...nowhere better to go, I followed for a pace, minding the

162

path's straight course from darkness into darkness. Thinking over the mind, process and hands which produced this way. What motive brought it about? What purpose did it serve? With every footstep here long removed by the wind, only my own senseless allegiance to precedent justifies a cause I can never know.

~

The desert is as sorry a companion for thought as it is for fraternity. I sometimes claim that my muse lives here, though this is a lie. Whatever sentience moves across the dark sands comes no further than the outskirts of my camp. I mistake its eyes reflected in my light for those of the fox who lived here first. Neither will come nearer than reflection, nor suggest more than aloof disinterest. The desert and the fox leave me to my own devices, to find thought and words on my own, caring for neither credit nor attribution.

~

A nondescript slice of concrete in the desert marks the spot where a small island of gas pumps once stood. I discovered the remains of this old Route 66 service station by studying satellite imagery of the desert around the ghost town of Siberia. While exploring the site, my mind contrived the story of human ambition and loss here which I suspect may bear more than fleeting resemblance to fact. And the ghosts I've borne in my mind for this place are now condemned to haunt these ruins for the rest of my days.

~

I discovered all that remains of the gas station and cafe at the California ghost town of Siberia. Sal and Ruth built this place in

163

the 20's out of mortar and desert sand. The combination home and business had two gas pumps and a service garage with a maintenance pit. There was a separate door into the cafe which had wooden floors, and where Ruth served her customers on fine decorated chinaware. When traffic on the old highway at last gave out, Ruth and Sal made the tough decision to leave their life's work behind to fall to ruin and fade into the desert, while the couple sought better fortune elsewhere. Today nothing remains of the gas station and cafe, but stone foundations and the outlines of lives now smothered in indifference.

~

I further found the stairs which led into the abandoned roadside diner at Siberia, California. How many road-weary American pilgrims stepped up and through the door here for a half hour of relief from the trials of crossing the harsh desert in an unreliable jalopy, or miners coming in from the surrounding claims for a welcome taste of civilization and a home-cooked meal. How many would-be Californians, like my own great-grandfather, came here dreaming of a better life if they could only get across this cursed desert! Is it possible my great granddad may have actually been here? Did he perhaps at one time step up these two steps to receive his first formal welcome into California after his long journey from Illinois? The places of rest were few at that time along this inhospitable stretch of America's Mother Road, making the odds he'd been here not unreasonable, nor very far-fetched.

~

High desert temperatures today kept me near Siberia, and far from the frontier where The Great Indifference doesn't loom. Why does it remain so far? Why can't it reclaim the ghost town

164

in the same way as the nocturnal fox who haunts my camp, or the ruin which spoils every human artifact here? It seems human absence is not enough. All reminder must be gone; save the living pulse of a solitary individual, far off trail, far from any comfort or aid, which is the only companionship The Great Indifference may ever abide. I wonder if I'll sense this strange absence just before the light of my life winks out? When my body is far off trail, beyond any comfort or aid—when the dark frontier grows near, and reality swells with dead promise. I suspect I will. I suspect that's how we all die, and the reason we cling so desperately to this wondrous thing of life; we sense that our living is something of a revolt, a strange and orderly uphill climb against the pull of universal disorder and chaos. The Great Indifference is that uncaring gravity well we hope to avoid by averting our eyes towards fellowship, love, and laughter; and by telling ourselves and one another comforting stories of reunion, reconciliation, and forgiveness. But the night doesn't care about our fear, nor the wind our chill, nor solitude our lonesome desperation. Better than stories is to face the night, stand in the wind, and embrace today the ones we love. Then, when we discover indifference looming with the intake of our final breath, we can close our eyes and smile peacefully at an inevitable reunion arrived at after a well lived life.

~

An early lunch in a Route 66 cemetery at the ghost town of Ludlow. Nearly all the graves here are unnamed, and assembled of scrape lumber and nails. Remembrance would be left to the imagination.

~

Today's desert adventure did yield a very pleasant surprise! In my youth my body could tolerate much heat and outdoor

165

exertion, with little impact besides a little weight loss and a propensity to go further than I should, resulting in many blind stumbles alone through darkened desert terrain after failing to find camp before sundown. Back then, I could go all day, and into the night, with little fatigue, and rarely dissuaded from any wilderness goal.

After returning to California from my life in Japan, I found my new desert adventures were commonly cut short due to sudden exhaustion, and a quite unfamiliar accompanying sense of fear over my physical well-being. I chocked this new limit up to my advancing age, and resigned myself to a fate of steadily diminishing horizons with each successive year.

And then came today. Wow! My old self has seemingly returned! At dawn I hiked a few miles out from the ghost town of Siberia, cautious of the summertime desert inferno I knew would soon arrive, and concerned my body might quickly give out with the heat, extreme exposure and exertion. By the time I returned from this first hike the heat was indeed on, and I'd greedily consumed all my water before I arrived back at camp. I should have been redlined, but I was ready to go out again. And I did!

After refilling my canteens, I struck out for round two, and an even longer and harder hike. By the time I was back again, the day was hotter, and the water was again no more, yet my body seemed ready to do it all over again. I held back though, not wanting to press too far into this surprising, rediscovered capability.

It's 4:30 PM now and the desert will soon begin to cool. I feel as lively and ready as I did at dawn, though the eight liters of water which I've today drank and sweat away have left my

166

exterior a sun-scorched, salty, dusty, and stinky mess. Just like when I was young!

How nice to meet my youthful self again out here in the summertime desert wastes. But don't worry. I won't be fooled. I'm 53, not 25. And no matter how good I may feel today I must always respect my true age and my body's true condition.

~

The desert around Siberia goes on tonight without me. Another dark passage of night like billions before, and billions to come. My presence so brief and fleeting and irrelevant as to escape notice of something with no capacity to notice. Such futile ends those delicious thoughts under the railway bridge. So meaningless to eternity my vain attempts at virtue. Still, I think. Still, I pursue virtue. For eternity was never mine. And relevance is found in each moment of common human connection. Let the universe go on, and pursue whatever mindless ends it holds with the patience of an immortal. Time was never mine. Just these moments. Just these words.

~

I'd bring others with me to the desert if I didn't already know that solitude would retreat before our advance.

~

The hot desert months protest my every ambition. Those far mountains...impossible. Those near hills...don't even think about it. A few days camping exposed upon the alluvium...maybe a day. Such dreams are reserved for winter. Though even then I sense mute protest to my every solitary excursion.

~

I previously believed that winter was the best season for desert hiking. Cold nights, snug in my good sleeping bag. Warm, temperate days, when I can walk for miles while drinking little and sweating less. But now I'm suspect summer has become my preferred time to hike in the desert. I'm not there for the walk after all, or the sights, or—heaven forbid!—any companionship. My aim is the limits. Which are much nearer and more distinct when the temperature is above 100 degrees (37 C.). A simple August walk a half mile from camp, while the inferno burns, and the landscape twists and shimmers with threat, goes as deep as a five-mile December excursion over black barren peaks, and through long twisting valleys of stone. Though I can turn and see camp, or the road, or my motorcycle, seemingly nearby under the summer sun, my mind presses such comforting thoughts aside with much concerned attention to my red, swelling hands, my nearly empty canteen, the total lack of any sheltering shade, and the onset of a woozy haze and dizziness, and faltering ability to see or think straight. Indifference looms then, surrounds, envelopes and ignores me as only its nature and capability demand. My skin then threatens to dry and crisp, and my bones to bleach and break, as my folly and insignificance are held like twin gifts in hands held upright in the direction of safely. This is what I sought with such difficulty in the winter wilds. This is what I found so easily in the summer desert, within footsteps of my car, when only I had the foresight to go alone, knew better, and went anyway.

~

Is it possible to will a place to become haunted? If so, then I suspect I succeeded this weekend during my visit to the desert ghost town of Siberia. The ghosts I made there are only as real

168

as the emotions I used to create them. And they followed me away from that place when I returned home, and will haunt my memory for as long as I live or care to recall. The ghosts will die with me, just like the prior passing of the real persons whose hidden history is their secret inspiration. But such is the way of hauntings, to derive from hinted facts, to then grow and live by imagination, until the imaginer themselves becomes nothing more than a faint and shadowy impression, an indistinct suggestion of facts, a muse and inspiration to the imagination of generations yet to come.

~

Go with a friend, to discover something you can share. Go alone, to find something you may be unable to share.

~

A stone wall is all that remains of the old railroad station at Siberia. The stones which make up the wall were pulled by the builders from surrounding desert alluvium; and represent well the long and diverse geologic history of the region. The stones include layered sedimentary rocks formed when this place was the bottom of a shallow sea. There's pink rhyolite which flowed from a nearby volcano. One stone includes course breccia from an ancient landslide or waterfall. While still another is a lovely conglomerate formed at the bottom of a deep pool at the end of a long series of rapids, perhaps in the age of dinosaurs. Though the wall itself represents very recent events in human history, the stones and sand of which it is made tell a much older and more interesting story. This same story is told by the desert itself. If only we have eyes to see.

~

Warming my hands by this small fire. The dark and vacant desert night crowds close with its silent depth. There's little fuel left. Just a few small sticks from someone else who'd been here. Where are they now? There are no lights in the night. It seems I'm truly alone. But that's always been the case. Even in a crowd, my flame—like the flame of all others—burns at the discretion of just my attendance. The fuel is not the matter. There's plenty of that. It's the attendance, and the effort I make, to pile on more fuel, and stir the coals. But now my arms grow weak, as they've been doing for years, since about age forty. And my thoughts a little slow, and stray, forgetful even...to tend the fire. That's why it's become so small. Just a dimming light in the infinite night. I'm tired now. It's time for a rest. I'll just lay down here on the soft sand. It's warm from the day which has already passed. A comforting reminder of the life that was. I'll just close my eyes for a bit. The fire seems fine. I'm sure the coals will still be glowing at dawn. The night always ends well. That's always what I've said.

~

Walking in the mountains of Japan consumed my mind in direct proportion to the distance moved. If I walked five miles, then my mind was never further than that same distance. No place then was really very wild, even though I sometimes went where I suspect nobody'd ever been.

Desert miles stretch all out of proportion to distance. Five miles or fifty are to the same effect. Even fifty yards can do the job when conditions are right.

Lately it seems I don't even need to go. Just remembering the desert is becoming enough. That never happened with the mountains, or the sea, or with solitude alone.

I'm tempted to think the desert is coming for me. Has me trapped in some way. But that's nonsense. Indifference doesn't care. Is incapable of giving a damn. It's all in my mind. My vain attempt to hold on to what I've found. To gain some purchase in reality that might survive my passing. But the desert doesn't care. Nor the mountains. Nor solitude. Though the desert voices this silence the loudest.

~

That look on the old man's face. Even though we were both at a crowded mall, surrounded by effervescent living. A warm summer evening. Crowds of young people living. Did he see the indifference? Was that why his gaze went past everyone into nothing? I think he did. He doesn't need the desert. He's almost there.

~

I wrote recently of tending a campfire. However, it's been years since I've actually built one. I prefer now to let darkness come on its own when I'm alone in the wild. I'll use a light to set up camp, or a flame to cook my meal. But when the camp is set, and my stomach is full, I'll switch off the light, and sit alone in the vast darkness. Almost like before.

~

I asked myself today why my thoughts so often turn to death, and the related subjects of emptiness, indifference, and oblivion. It's because I enjoy life, and I believe there's nothing

171

to follow after we die. I believe that what waits after death is the same utter void we didn't know before we were born. I believe all this love and laughter, challenge and struggle, and the many opportunities to be, and to do good, will pass away completely the instant our mind shuts off, and our being begins to dissolve away. I believe there will be no chance for reunion, reconciliation, or justice after our functions cease. And I believe that we will never again awake into anything like what we are now, though our matter and energy may in fact be used by others. So, if this is what I believe, then I guess it's no wonder I spend a lot of time thinking about, and gazing into, the void. No wonder I go to wild places. That's why I choose the desert. And the reason I always go alone. For whenever I return from such places, or such thoughts, I always come back a better man. More sober and composed. Less troubled by petty things. More engaged with my family. More at ease with who I am. Better resolved towards being a good man. And more prepared for the absolute end I must very soon face...alone.

~

Just one more week until the start of flash flood season in the California desert. Soon my dark and silent nights in Siberia will come alive with thunder, lightning, and rain in the nearby Bristol Mountains. These summer storms create powerful and short-lived rivers, which appear suddenly from nowhere, to spill from canyons and dissipate across the broad alluvial plain where I sleep. The floods carry heavy sediment loads of course rock and sand, which are deposited atop the desert, adding new layers to a geologic story which began 34 million years ago; in a period when grasslands first appeared on Earth, and rainforests retreated to the equator. The story goes on, year upon year, century after century, for countless millennia, with few observers, and nobody to know the full tale.

172

~

There are two types of "swim into deep water" that I enjoy in my life. The first is any solo adventure which stretches the bounds of safety; and puts me beyond easy reach of help. I enjoy these experiences for the impression of frail vulnerability I gain whenever I'm all alone with The Great Indifference; and have no friend or comfort to turn to.

The second "swim into deep water" is when I find some way to honestly undermine my own beliefs, or anything else which I think is true. Sadly, this is becoming less easy, now that I've killed so much of my world view, and am left with only a handful of "I dunno"s. It seems there's little existential threat to admitted ignorance, though there's lots of discomfort if you don't like not knowing, and find yourself all alone with your doubt. But then that's where the first and second types of "deep water" meet, and where we enter the very deep water which I call the "Deep End of the Ocean".

The Deep End of the Ocean is where admitted ignorance and accepted indifference come together and cancel one another out. The very deep sea grows still here in the face of the fact that we don't really know the answer we might previously have thought so sure, while simultaneously recognizing that the universe does not, or is incapable of, giving a damn about our troubling dilemma.

I don't get to swim in deep water very often, as life has a way of sending rescuers to such places to quickly extract and return us back to work, or to our friends, or our family, our church, bar, shopping mall, television, or anything else that gives us comforting suckle, while reassuring us that we are right, and in fact, not alone.

173

So, I'll take such swims as I can, and when I'm able. And with a little luck I'll one day drown out there, far to sea, alone with my doubt, beyond any savior, trembling within the dark, indifferent depths above, below, and everywhere all around.

~

The most disturbing thing about being alone in the desert isn't what you might find there, but what you won't.

~

The volcanoes of the Eastern Mohave Desert are largely extinct due to the way in which they were formed. Each cinder cone and lava dome in this region had its origin deep within the Earth's upper mantle. This geologic story begins roughly 100 miles northeast of the intersection of the North American and Pacific crustal plates—which form the San Andreas Fault— where this fault crosses the San Bernardino Mountains at Cajon Pass. Though these plates are running laterally against one another, there is sufficient subduction of the Pacific plate to draw water-rich oceanic crust deep into the mantle below the North American plate. The introduction of water into the mantle at these depths lowers pressure such that large bubbles of hot magma form which begin to rise up and into the Earth's solid crust. It's essentially the same process which causes bubbles to form in a bottle of pop after the cap is opened. These "bubbles" of molten rock burn their way slowly through miles of solid rock as they rise towards the surface, cooling, changing, and growing smaller as they go. Tens of thousands of years later, the molten bubbles of magma arrive at the surface to "pop" as small, short-lived volcanoes, or simply to bulge through the surface—without popping—to form nicely symmetrical lava domes.

While driving through the desert on Interstates 15, 40, or old Route 66, it's possible to see dozens of these extinct volcanoes and lava domes frozen at the moment of their death, when the last of their molten magma cooled upon reaching the surface of the Earth. We can even gauge how long their journey was by the color and texture of their rocks; with dark volcanoes rising more quickly than light-colored volcanoes which enjoyed a longer, or slower, trip from the molten mantle to the surface of the Earth.

~

Forty-eight hours until I leave again for Siberia. It's a swim into deep water out there at this time of year, even at night. A warm glide over unfathomed depths in every direction. Sometimes out there I distract myself with living. It's an easy trick which we learn from birth. But the game becomes so apparent the moment I falter in my play. Like a man playing solitaire on a desert island, who suddenly looks up and remembers his real situation. There are no conspirators when I'm alone out there in the deep desert. Nobody to help keep up the game. No one to share the illusion. None at all...out there.

~

If you don't enjoy criticism, then don't attempt to swim alone in the deep desert. If you don't like being wrong, then remain at home with your costly peace and certitude. I'd accept no something in exchange for my nothing. The desert took it all away from me, including the space where it once all belonged.

~

I arrived at Siberia minutes after sundown; and had only a short amount of time to set up camp before deep darkness

175

enveloped the land. The only light or sound of humanity after nightfall here is the very rare passing of a vehicle on Route 66, or the commanding passage of a mile-long train moving up or down the Mojave Grade. The mountains to the south are 16 miles (26 kilometers) away. During summer thunderstorms I sometimes see lightning in those mountains, without hearing any sound of thunder.

~

Silence and peace with every footstep and moment. Even now the desert quiet is with me. This has nothing to do with the desert, really. Though without the deep desert the spell might never have been broken. I used to worry that if I spent too much time alone out there then I'd in some way never get back. Instead, what I've found out there has seemingly become lost within me. It looks out through my eyes and sees the vast and terrible emptiness behind everything, reminding me...to build and maintain sound principles of virtue, which are the tools and apparatus of a good and meaningful life. It hushes my mind with quiet when life rustles with demand, helping me to focus and attend to my responsibility, as well as the true ends of virtue. I see the nothing which awaits after life is done, which fact compels me to act now in the name of virtue, and the improved well-being of my fellows, as well as the well-being of those yet to come. I used to think I'd someday lose myself in the desert. Though I never guessed I'd be lost until the desert indifference became lost in me.

~

90-minute countdown to departure for Siberia. I wonder if that fear I always meet along the way is waiting now to ambush me? It usually lurks out past Ludlow, not far from Pisgah crater, on the right side of Route 66.

When the fear comes it always tracks me close beside the road, easily shadowing the big bike as I roll and glide through the black lava fields. In winter, it's dark already when I arrive, so I can't see, but I know it's there. In summer, like now, it seems to move stealthily among the rocks while waiting for nightfall, which approaches fast from the east.

The fear does something to me about three miles from Siberia—where I always want to turn back. Haven't yet. But who knows tonight? Turning in onto the dirt road to the Siberia ruins, I've more important and real worries to attend to; as navigating a 600-pound motorcycle on a dirt road is real fear enough to dispel any mere phantom.

Once I arrive, and shut off the bike, the fear is gone. It wasn't like that the first, or even the second time I went—when I cowered in the car, with the doors locked, staring out at the dark. I felt like such a kid then. It's a wonder I went back. No more though. When the bike's engine stops. And the desert silence swarms in. All fear. Every last bit. Drains away.

~

Have I arrived in Siberia or has Siberia arrived in me?

~

Greetings from Siberia. It's dark now. And big. This place is so big. As I sit here on the hot, dark sand, I think I've figured something out. I know now why this place can't get me. Why I'm not afraid here anymore. Why the solitude and the night, and the indifference, can't take me away; though it's got me now, and there's nowhere to run. It's because I'm connected— deeply connected. To my wife, and my daughter, and my brother, and my mom. And to the others too. I try hard with

177

my family. And I do a pretty good job, I think. Not so much the others. It's my failing. One of many. These connections though do the trick, I think. They keep me safe here. Prevent my mind from wandering to places from which it might never return.

In 1989 I left my girlfriend—now my wife—behind in a small college town near Oregon while I embarked on a Great Life Adventure. I made it as far as the desert. In fact, not far from where I am now. Just over the Bristol mountains to the northwest, near the west shore of Soda Dry Lake. Something happened to me then which caused me to promptly return to Yumiko. I gave up the desert then. I knew I was about to go too far into the wild. Not physically. But that other way. I sensed then—quite rightly—that if I'd continued then I'd never have made it back. I was right. I know that now.

Now I'm back in the desert—twenty-eight years later. The same threat looms here like before. I can sense it. But I'm not afraid. It can't get me. I'm too strong now. Though my body is weak, my spirit, resolve and hard-won maturity are more than a match for The Great Indifference.

Not so in my youth. If I'd stayed, then I would surely have been consumed.

~

I don't expect to remember life.

~

Every swim into deep water comes at a price. The cost is the genuine quality of our connection with those we left behind. For as our universe expands without them, we find we've less to

178

relate, and have fewer common connections. That's why we so often choose society over solitude, institutions over independence, and the status quo over the strange and the unknown. Venture too far or long into deep water and we risk losing sight of shore. The place where you swim then is very real, it just won't seem so to others, and the things you describe...well, perhaps it's better you just keep these things to yourself. Enjoy your society, relish your institutions, abide the status quo if it be good, and just, and of virtue. Just don't forget where you've been. And what you've seen.

~

At one point during my hike in the desert today I took refuge from the heat under a bridge where Route 66 crosses a desert wash. I found a Japanese book under the bridge. The book describes a 'round-the-world bicycle journey. Hand-written Japanese writing on the back of the book read "I will not die far from home. I will make it back alive." Yumiko tells me the writing is a man's handwriting, and the language in a style of the Kansai region of Japan.

~

My book should draw like vacuum and drain like death.

~

Take another with you if all you want is adventure. Life can pass easy this way. Though I suspect at times you'll wonder if there's more. There isn't. Which is an awful fact. Quick. Cover it up with distraction. Turn back to the comfort of friends. Clasp your hands in prayer. Keep yourself company with the sound of your own voice. Just don't go alone. Unless you really want to see.

~

Though I missed the mark yesterday in the desert—failed to disconnect, failed to become lost—I did however find trace of someone else's success. That Japanese man who left his book beneath a Route 66 bridge. The boldly scribbled note he left at the back of the book. There's no doubt he met The Great Indifference. It's not just in my mind. It's really not out there.

~

My goal from last weekend's hike was to safely explore how many hours I could hike into the day after sunrise, and before things started to get dangerous. The answer is about four hours on a day when temps will max out at around 110 degrees Fahrenheit (43 C). But that was WITH three stops to rest under various flash flood bridges beneath the railroad tracks and Route 66. These stops were crucial to bringing my body temperature down, as there is absolutely no other shade in the open desert to use for this purpose. If I hadn't had those bridges to rest under, I think the hike could have been only two hours or less. I could literally feel my body temperature rising like a kettle on the stove while walking exposed to the direct sunlight. This was especially true after 9:00 AM. The experience was rather alarming, and I definitely would not want to be caught an hour or more from camp during summer any time after 9:00 AM. I must keep the summertime hiking to either nighttime or for just a few hours after dawn. A VERY good lesson learned.

~

I've found what's possibly another lost grave belonging to the desert ghost town of Siberia. The only reason I even guess it's a grave is because it matches so well with graves I've seen in other ghost towns along Route 66. This collection of arranged stones is located just a short way out from where the town used to be, is formed of hastily arranged stones, and can seemingly serve no other useful purpose. Wooden crosses or headstones were commonly used on graves like this, though desert winds take their toll on such markers, and many graves I've seen are today missing their wooden markers, and remain just a pile or outline of stones. I was a little delirious with the heat when I found this, and I'm afraid I probably couldn't find it again if I tried.

~

I'm following that mysterious stone-lined desert path which runs from nowhere to nowhere within the desert ghost town of Siberia. This path has become a companion of sorts for me whenever I come here, as I always seem to stumble upon it during my nighttime walks, and I still find new traces of it when I meander about in the morning drinking my coffee. Invariably, my mind always wonders about the hands which so carefully placed these.

~

I wish I had the courage to write all of the words. I'd have thought it would be easier way out here. Maybe after I lose sight of land? Maybe only after I toss the compass over the side?

Route 66 camp at Siberia, California: It's summer now, and already I can feel the intensity of the sun as it crawls up slowly towards the horizon. The solar heat literally spills over the mountains before the sun can even be seen. It's like feeling the first trickle of a heat flood which is about to engulf the desert. I get a little anxious in this hour of the day, and I tend to work fast to break camp and ready the motorcycle for a hasty retreat. The radiant heat energy of the desert is astounding, and there is absolutely nowhere to hide besides the shade under railroad and highway bridges, which I sometimes share with birds and jackrabbits. It's no wonder most of the animal life out here is nocturnal, hiding away from the sun at dawn, just before the inferno switches on. Walking alone across the desert on a summer day can be a very lonesome experience. Where is everyone? Why are all the locals hiding? What do they know that I don't seem to grasp?

Ready to depart Siberia California: The night before was especially hot, only cooling to a comfortable level just before dawn. I ate my dinner while seated on the gravelly dirt, covered in sweat, wondering about male tarantulas which wander actively through the summer night looking for females. Though the wind was gentle this particular night, I did take precaution to lash the tent securely to the ground with pegs and ropes, and to angle the tent with the narrow sides facing east and west, which align the tent perpendicular to the night wind, which can sometimes rise suddenly to blow with great intensity for hours through the night. Desert night winds (unless due to a storm) nearly always blow into the desert, which means west to east at Siberia, which fact allows me to reliably prepare my tent to weather the blast, should it come.

The night is quiet here in every season, except the trains, which literally blast through the dark with deep rumbling engines which shake the ground, and resonant whistle blasts which echo off the black volcanoes. The stars also remain constant in every season. Even when the Bristol and Bullion mountains to the north and south are being drenched in summer thunderstorms, the air overhead at Siberia is nearly always clear and clean all the way to the Milky Way. Just satellites mar the view, or an occasional jetliner, strangely silent, remind me of my species.

It's a good thing. Such solitude. So much is lost then. So little gained. A very equitable trade.

~

Eventually, I won't need the desert. Or the silence. Or the stillness. Or the atmosphere of peace. Maybe then I'll understand the reason Emerson wrote that "the wise man stays at home."

~

With today's outing, I was experimenting with how long I could remain exposed and moving out in the open desert, on a day when temps would top out at around 110 degrees F. (43 C.). I learned that I don't want to be more than an hour away from shade after approximately 8:00 AM. I could probably extend that range by wearing more—and better quality—clothing, as it seems it's really the exposure to direct sunlight which drives my body temperature up fast, rather than the simple fact of being outdoors. The sunlight hitting my exposed skin seems to transfer an astonishing amount of heat energy, which might otherwise be blocked or deflected by a sensible layer of clothing. I'm planning to research the desert clothing solutions

183

in use by desert-dwelling peoples in places like Africa and the Middle East for some tips and tricks to help keep me safe. Another idea is to carry some form of easy-to-assemble shelter which I can quickly erect as a hiding place from the sun. I'm thinking perhaps of using a large, reflective space blanket secured to the ground with pegs, and elevated with a short pole. For this journey, I was using the very nice shady areas beneath flash flood bridges along both the railroad and Route 66. I'm certain I could easily spend an entire day under one of these bridges during even the hottest desert days. However, a smaller shelter (like my proposed space-blanket tent) would likely offer far less cooling opportunity, and I'll need to experiment carefully with such options. An extra concern is the fact that since I'm on a motorcycle, there's no chance to escape the heat in a pinch by ducking into a car to enjoy the air conditioning. This means that I must always plan to get back to my bike with enough exposure reserves (new term?) to get the big GSA fired up, safely down the dirt road from Siberia, and out onto Route 66 where I can enjoy the moderately cooling effect of a 60+ MPH wind. Altogether, I'm very satisfied with this experiment, though I think the heat may have made me a bit delirious at times.

~

I'm beginning to assemble some going alone best practices; suggestions for anyone interested in entering wildness alone in search of The Great Indifference. Of course, the first trick is knowing that you don't need to go to wildness to encounter indifference. You simply need to see past the thin veneer of meaning and illusory permanence we so expertly smear over everything and everyone around us.

1. *Go alone—but return to someone you love*
   Reject all company in the wild. Reject even the desire to

consult yourself. Let every new outing put yet another mile between you and everything that comforts and reassures your mind. With time, what you've left behind will be like a distant carnival of stimulation and distraction. A loud, brilliant spectacle of days leading to a fearful end few dare honestly consider or discuss. But beware going too far, too soon, or too young. For it is possible to go so distant into wildness that you can never get back—even if you find your way back.

2. *Go alone—but find love in your life*
   Find a partner who will understand, and who will be comfortable with you going to the wild alone; someone to come back to; someone who will leave a light on for your return, and who will warm you with their embrace when you reach out longingly to hold them after you've returned. Someone to appreciate after you've seen what's not really out there. It's not necessary that this person share your interest in such solitude, or understand your reasons. It's enough that they accept this part of who you are, and do not dissuade your reasonable pursuit of going alone. So, when dating, be up front about this thing you do; tell your potential partner about your practice of sometimes going alone to places off the map. While dating, engage in going alone, mark the calendar with your scheduled outings, and describe your plans. Consider wisely if this person cannot tolerate your solitary bent and trajectory.

   I'll include now a quote to illustrate my point about partnering with someone who can help us stay grounded, though I hesitate doing so for fear this quote may be misunderstood. I'm not adding this to suggest the poet should necessarily find a non-poet or more domestic soul to share their life with, but only to point out what others have observed, and which my own experience has borne

185

witness. Let me share then a short passage from Nathaniel Hawthorn's extraordinary novel, The House of the Seven Gables. In this particular section of the book we learn about the platonic relationship between the old man Clifford, and his young niece Phoebe. Clifford, being of the poetic sort, and someone lost to the world in a reality he can neither share nor make very real; and Phoebe, a young woman of grounded sentiment, made buoyant of her youth, practicality, and common sense. Phoebe brings a peace and fulfillment to Clifford's life, which is all out-of-proportion to anything he could offer the girl; though she does gain somewhat through the administration of her native charity and benevolence. The benefit of relations between the two is quite one-sided due to Clifford's advanced age and degraded mental prowess, though perhaps if he'd had someone like Phoebe in his youth, he might not have become so very lost, and she might too have gained from the unique qualities and gifts Clifford might have been in better position to share:

> *"Now, Phoebe's presence made a home about her,—that very sphere which the outcast, the prisoner, the potentate,—the wretch beneath mankind, the wretch aside from it, or the wretch above it,—instinctively pines after,—a home! She was real! Holding her hand, you felt something; a tender something; a substance, and a warm one: and so long as you should feel its grasp, soft as it was, you might be certain that your place was good in the whole sympathetic chain of human nature. The world was no longer a delusion.*

> *By looking a little further in this direction, we might suggest an explanation of an often-suggested mystery. Why are poets so apt to choose their mates, not for any similarity of poetic endowment, but for qualities*

which might make the happiness of the rudest
handicraftsman as well as that of the ideal craftsman
of the spirit? Because, probably, at his highest
elevation, the poet needs no human intercourse;
but he finds it dreary to descend, and be a stranger."

-Nathaniel Hawthorn

3. No campfire
    *Let the night come on its own terms. Sit alone on the hard
    ground and let darkness arrive. Walk blind into the night.
    Stumble and fall. And meet the fearful things you imagine
    are there. Return to your campsite both master and
    mastered.*

4. No seat
    *Never bring any chair into the wild. Nor create a seat. Just
    sweep away with your bare hand the larger stones and then
    sit on the ground, or in the sand, or on a rock. Or better
    yet, stand and move always.*

5. Find a desert
    *Go someplace hard and empty. Avoid places with soft
    grass on the ground, or green leafy trees for shade. Find
    someplace where no one goes. Find a place hot, or cold, or
    windy, or bleak. A place where life isn't easy or welcome.
    Where existence is hard. Where you perceive threat in the
    empty.*

6. No connectivity
    *Switch off the device. And then never turn it back on. Or,
    if your muse is catalyzed by sharing, then make the effort
    one way. Avoid checking or responding while in the wild.
    Or better yet, ever. Avoid curating both your experience*

and your life.

7. *No books*
   You know better. Leave the books at home. Though bring blank pages. And a pencil. Or your blog. Do these things if you discover your muse meets you there in the wastes. Listen and record what you hear then. Don't be embarrassed to share. Though you'll likely be looked at and thought of as increasingly odd if you do so honestly.

8. *Consider death at first light*
   Greet the dawn by imagining your own death, and the deaths of your loved ones, and the eternity of utter empty to follow for each of you. Imagine that you'll never again see the ones you love, nor they you. Never again experience any thought or emotion. Ask yourself how you should best spend the coming day, cognizant how few days really remain, and how much you will very soon utterly lose when this life is done.

~

I'm gearing up now for today's ride and overnight at Siberia. The temperature forecast is 109 degrees (43 C.) and 113 (45) for tomorrow. I always lose more in the desert than I gain. I wonder how much less there'll be of me after I return? I wonder what part of me will evaporate away today and tomorrow in the heat and empty?

~

I have a home. I have a wife. I have a daughter. And I have an extended family. And I have a place called Siberia. It's someplace that reminds me that the universe doesn't care. It's a place that threatens without acknowledging my presence. Its silence deafens my every hope and ambition. I become almost nothing here. For a night. And then a day. Before I go back to my wife. And to my daughter. And my family. And my life. And I resolve then to make purpose and meaning where there is none. To identify virtue and make it my friend. And to vow allegiance to what is true. And to deny what is false. And to live a Good Life. A life of meaning. A life of love. A life well lived.

~

I'm embarking on my first ever solo night hike in the desert. It's dark out there. And I've no reliable way to find my way back to a ghost town without lights or any sign of life. I won't go far this first time. Just until I can no longer touch bottom.

~

The temperature today was around 110 degrees F. (43 C.), with a gentle, yet very hot, wind blowing in from the west. It's hard to describe well the emptiness out here at night, with just my little penlight providing a dull haze of illumination in an ocean of black. The locomotives do thunder through from time to time, yet they seem as indifferent to my meek presence here as the night and the heat. I think it's their steel rails which insulate the occupants from the fearful reality which swims here in the night.

~

A lot of me evaporated away into the hot desert night during this hike. I'm discovering that the stuff that goes wasn't necessary anyway. Each time I go to the desert, I return with less. And I'm a better man for the loss. More deliberate. More sincere. Less distracted. Lighter in every way.

189

~

The desert quiet is everywhere with me now. Everything slower. Silence deep within the mind.

~

Desert skies offer little impediment to elevated thought. Without clouds, or much insulating humidity between the Earth and the vacuum of space, my thinking floats easily up and away from whatever might otherwise restrain and constrain upon the firm bedrock of convention. If I float my ideas high enough, I can no longer make out the ground. Everything becomes a vast landscape of indifference. There's little difference in any direction. Even the deep dark above yawns awesome and deep. A similar infinity below towards the ground. And around me on every side. I'm increasingly mute whenever I return. There seems little reason to share what I can barely find words to describe.

~

There'll be just a sliver of moon two days hence when I arrive at Siberia. The moon will hang low in the west just after I arrive at sunset. Within two hours this faint source of light will pass over the horizon, leaving deep night until dawn. A darkness not even the abundant starlight can awaken. I'll walk then alone into the desert. A flashlight to guide the way. All inner light extinguished through a force of will to fit in.

~

I'm at the edge of the desert now. Terrible heat. Awful, really. I've been exposed now for hours. So much has been drained from me. I'm counting the remaining hours now to sunset.

Anticipating some relief after the sun goes down. I like life this way. I enjoy looking over the awful edge of oblivion.

~

After nine months and four attempts I was at last able yesterday to get a San Bernardino County Sheriff's Deputy to the desert location where I discovered what I thought were human bones. Three deputies agreed, and the bones are now on their way to the coroner.

~

Have you ever smelled the odor of a rock? This is something I've only ever experienced in the deep East Mojave Desert. In the low, crumbling ruins of the ancient Bristol and Bullion mountains. Among the island peaks of the Old Dad and Old Woman mountains. And at the rugged and exposed feet of the great Providence and Granite mountains. The smell of stone here can only be detected during the hottest days of summer, and only just after sundown, when the faint twilight grows and a swell of gratitude emerges that we've survived another inferno day. The exposed stones here are the ancient product of the collision of continents; white, red, and black in color, rich in silicon and iron. It's the iron we can seemingly smell. It's the same odor of our own fresh and copious blood. The taste of a bloody nose. Something about the long hot day and the sudden cessation of heat when the sun goes down appears to draw this same faint odor from the stones, from the landscape itself. It's a beautiful smell while it lasts. Strangely familiar. Wildly unexpected. As exotic and evocative as a rare perfume. Don't expect this aroma of iron from the forest, or the sea, or the desert sands. It's a product of bare and exposed and ancient desert mountains. A factor of deep heat and sudden cooling,

191

and the relief of survival, and the promise of night, and the chance of another day.

~

I often like to compare my desert outings to a swim in the sea. In wintertime, a walk into the desert is like a leisurely swim into deep water from a calm and serene shoreline. It isn't until you're very far out that it dawns on you how deep, black and cold the water below is, and how distant the shimmering shore. In summertime though, a walk into the desert is like playing in the surf on a day when heavy wind and waves pound upon the shore. There's trepidation from the first step. And danger even before we're over our heads in apparent depth.

~

Summer is like a storm upon the desert. A raging tempest of heat, which drives nearly all life to the cover of shade, or to flee altogether until the storm's autumn end. To swim then is to risk death in short order. To drown in the heat. To die with bulging eyes and swollen tongue, stumbling naked towards a shimmering mirage. To become parched and bleached bones upon the sand.

The winter desert kills with cold indifference. It's cool daylight silence lures us too far from where we should turn back. The comfort is a feign illusion. Just a little further... I'll go just past that ridge... The atmosphere so mild and comforting at mid-afternoon. The sunset coming on. Shall I stop and watch? Nightfall. The onset of sudden, deep cold. Which way back? No lights. No trail. No guide. A final evening. The start of an endless night.

192

~

*There was a storm raging all about me during today's hike.
Invisible, for the clear, clean atmosphere, the dead air, and the
deceptive desert silence. Yet apparent in my beet-red face;
detectable in the real and rising anxiety of my fast words, and
the growing delirium evident in my odd topics of conversation,
and the distracted nature of my discourse with the camera. I'd
been exposed in the open sun in temperatures of 110-degree
Fahrenheit (43 C.) for over two hours, and the heat stress was
really beginning to take its toll. I remember thinking—while I
walked to hide under a Route 66 bridge—how I was perhaps
getting near to someplace bad with regard to my bodily
condition; getting close to someplace I shouldn't want to go.
Yet curiosity urged me to continue just a little further when I
soon left the shelter of the bridge. To inch just a bit nearer the
edge of heat stroke, and the one-way vista beyond. There's
something deeply satisfying about tempting danger in this way. I
suspect it's the same feeling others get when they drive very
fast, or swim with sharks, or climb without ropes. A deep
invigoration and appreciation of life which comes of every near
miss of life's final and utterly conclusive end.*

~

*The season of heat is passing. Temperatures today in the
Eastern Mojave Desert won't climb past 100 degrees (38 C.)
until mid-afternoon. A mild day by recent standards. Soon the
sun will relent its terrible onslaught of energy upon the land;
not by nature of diminished output, but only through the
gradual shortening of days, and indirect angle of attack. I can
already feel the coming change; anticipate the cooler evenings,
and the crisp bite of midnight cold which is herald of the much
deeper and colder winter nights to come. There isn't much
time between seasons here. Barely a chance to rest a moment*

*and prepare for the next season's atmosphere and inclination.
Spring and autumn are bliss here. Though the memory and
forecast of what was and what's to come dull all but the most
senseless immediate regard.*

~

*Age 53 and my mental faculties are both optimally tuned and
failing fast. The experience of operating this system is like
piloting an airplane through a range of mountains I can't
possibly summit. With each passing year of life, the canyons
narrow, and the valleys rise. There's no going back...and time's
running out ahead. I'd better do my thinking now before this
journey very soon ends as a smoldering stain upon a high
alpine cliff.*

~

*There is great virtue in self-destruction. By this I do not mean
self-harm; or injury in any way to our well-being, or our innate
sense of happiness. In fact, I seek to increase these greatly; to
rarefy goodness and find more immediate and sound answers
to life's most challenging issues and questions. I do this through
destruction. Self-destruction to be exact.*

*I attempt this destruction daily. Usually in the morning. Just
before sunrise. I do this by throwing everything of real value
upon the fire. Not a scrape of sentiment should remain. I start
the fire with a sincere question: are these things true? I then
heap on the fuel of criticism. Blow the flames with puffs of
objectivity. Lay on abundant dry honesty. And then watch the
new day's inferno rage.*

*What's left in the embers are the little bits of truth I'll carry for
another day. These are my treasures now. Not those*

194

combustible ideas of dogma, tradition, and authority. I've burned them down again. As I will again tomorrow. And the day after that.

My secret goal is to one day have nothing left to burn. To be forced to go a day in utter doubt and confusion. Oh, what a blessing to walk in the company of an ignorance hard earned of education, and lost utterly to fearless naked doubt.

~

I used to be afraid of the desert for impractical reasons. I was afraid of the dark, and the solitude, and the questions which lurked there. These fears have largely passed. Now I'm afraid of more practical things; like the heat, and the cold, and the risk of going very far while very alone. But also, there's a new and very different fear that's rising. I began to sense it just recently; perhaps truly during this last outing two weeks back. It's the sense of the perception of a pathway emerging before me. An invisible route of my own making. A way opening up which I know I'll follow. I don't fear this direction for any reason other than I know that passage is one way, and utterly irrevocable.

~

48 hours 'till Siberia. I'll arrive half an hour after sunset. It'll be dark then. I'm thinking perhaps I'll leave the motorcycle at the ghost town ruins, and night hike immediately after I arrive. Instead of packing the motorcycle with camping gear, I'll prepare my three-day tactical bag; and wear it while riding all the way out to the desert. This is easy to do, as I can simply loosen the pack's shoulder straps and allow the bike's pillion seat to carry the pack's full weight. This way, when I arrive, I

195

simply get off the bike, tighten the straps, and start walking into the dark.

For this hike I'll go perhaps a mile north from Siberia into the near edge of the Deep-Water Wilderness. This will be my first real overnight in the desert—and away from the reassuring touch of civilization—in over three decades. A homecoming of sorts.

The last time I did a desert night hike like this I was very young. I remember that night well. I remember emerging from my tent deep in the night to admire the rising moon. I remember the warm empty promise of the desert night wind. I remember feeling so small and frail, standing naked and barefoot on the sand in the vast and empty night, the great, dark desert illuminated with faint pale moonlight, the only man on Earth it seemed. It's possible my nihilism can be traced to this moment, or moments like this. There were many then.

I wonder how my much older mind will react to this same experience 48 hours from now? Things are very different now. I'm a family man now. I have solid life objectives now. I have sound principles now. I have deeply meaningful purpose now. I know and recognize The Great Indifference now. I don't fear the empty. Death is a wondrous, perhaps utterly final mystery to me now. I no longer pretend I've out-thought death's mystery, and I no longer pledge allegiance to any comforting story of forever. I now instead await and welcome whatever strange, wondrous, or terrible reality really awaits. I think I'm ready for whatever I'll now find or not find in the night.

~

There's always lightning here during the summer at night in Siberia. In the east. And in the north. Ever seen. Never heard.

196

~

*There was an enormous dust storm racing across the desert
towards me. I was scrambling to set up and secure my tent
before the storm arrived. The initial winds were intense, nearly
knocking the tent flat before blotting out the remaining sun and
ushering in the start of a long, hot, gritty night.*

*The dust storm hit my desert camp before I could finish
pounding in the last tent stakes, flapping the loose tent madly,
while minute particles of dust began clouding the sun and
irritating my eyes. The wind blew hard for several hours at the
start of night, while I alternated resting and walking about the
dark camp. It was too hot to remain in the tent. Too windy to
cook a meal or relax. Too soon for sleep.*

*The wind eventually stopped. The dust passed or settled into
the dark. The stars came out. Still too hot to sleep well, I
bound the tent flaps open, to invite in the night breeze, as well
as scorpions, tarantula, and snakes. I lay naked upon the floor
of the tent. Nothing to sleep on or covering me; just the soft,
hot sand below, and the dehydrating hot wind above, blowing
heat all about and over every inch of my body.*

*I slept then. Not well. Not deep. Night thoughts rose in my
mind between dream and consciousness. I tended these like a
small, fragile flame when I could; when my mind rose far
enough from sleep to realize I was thinking. I let all those quiet
night thoughts go. I can't remember a one now. They were
ghosts in the night.*

*I'm awake now. It's another hour before dawn. The morning
wind woke me with a long and sudden blast of heat. I expect
this is how the desert anticipates the summer day to come. An
anxiety of mindless natural force.*

197

The desert around me is so dark and empty. Only the wind my companion. And the stars a distant, mute audience. This night I'll remember always. A fitting candidate for the someday smile on an old man's face; my grandchildren wondering...why does granddad smile that way?

~

Sweat and life evaporate equally out here. The lull and comfort of civilization and companionship dull my perception of life's immediate passing. The tick, tick of seconds we'll never get back.

Don't think such thoughts! Here, amuse yourself with the TV, or watch a movie. How about a meal? Or a drink? Or a chat with friends?

There's no such distraction out here. Just the locomotive's determined passing; blind to anything other than their rails.

I can't help sense time's passage here. Feel the very real weight of age. My muscles seem to fade with each step. That distant peak; possible yesterday, impossible today, not even a dream tomorrow.

Each moment, less and less.

~

It didn't escape my notice that the desert dust storm I encountered two nights back encompassed the Deep-Water Wilderness. Before the wind and sand swallowed me up where I camped on the gently sloping alluvial plain near Siberia, I watched as the storm-front passed quickly across The Edge of Deep-Water, one mile to the north of my camp. This means the dust storm swept up and through, first the twisting red canyons of Deep-Water, and then along the craggy black volcanic mountains leading to the heart of the desolate Bristol range. From within those mountains, someone would never see such a storm approaching.

The experience of such a sandstorm within the mountains would be both sudden, and overwhelming. Immediately prior, the air would be still. The sky would be clear. The desert as silent as always...and then suddenly a brown wall and wave of wind would appear over the ridge and up the canyon. Anyone walking or setting up camp there would be consumed in seconds by wind and sand; left standing or hunkering against the sandblast gale. Eyes covered by hands. Mouth tight. Mind racing. And as these storms often come at twilight, the person caught so exposed would also be subject to sudden nightfall, as the sand snuffs out the setting sun, ushering in a long, harsh twilight.

I wonder how often the desert explorers and miners of old encountered such storms? The only story I've read of such an event relates a 100-year-old tale of an old miner who was caught suddenly by a sandstorm in the same general area where I was camping two nights back. In fact, he was a few miles southeast at the edge of the Amboy Crater lava field, attempting the long walk from Bagdad to Twentynine Palms where he would attempt to sell various items he'd collected from the mines. He was an old man; and got by any way he could. I suspect the sandstorm he met rose up from the same dry lakebed where my storm was born. The miner was overwhelmed by the storm—just as I was—and sought shelter in a lava tube, while I found refuge in a tent. While waiting out the wind and sand he discovered large chunks of gold in the lava. The story goes that he took enough gold to fill a Bull Durham bag, with plans to return for the rest. Sadly, the old miner was dead within 24 hours of his return to Bagdad, and the gold he brought back was used to pay his funeral expense.

I expect these sandstorms have been a feature of the desert here for tens of thousands of years. Now that I know of them—and know what to look for and expect—I'll anticipate the day I'm once again suddenly enveloped in a long, blustery, gritty night of blowing sand and howling wind. I'll relish the chance; and prepare my mind for the opportunity.

~

Four weeks back and my overnight at Siberia was a brutal affair. The ground had absorbed a great deal of energy from sunlight, which it then radiated into the cooling night air from sundown until well past midnight. Sleep was very difficult then, as sweat pooled on the bottom of my tent, and I tossed and turned until 3:00 AM. I arose at dawn thoroughly dehydrated, and fully sapped of all energy. The prospect of facing sunrise, and the broiling day to come, was daunting then, and I hastily broke camp in favor of a full retreat to my cool and comfortable home on the coast.

Two weeks later, on August 11th, and the story was different. Temperatures were five degrees cooler, and the Earth was losing its collected daytime heat fast after sundown. This was due to an unexpected sandstorm which rose suddenly at dusk, with winds that seemingly drained the Earth of heat before the long summer twilight was complete. I slept better then, save for the clamor of wind rattling my tent, and the grit of sand blowing in through open flaps, as well as the bite of some desert creepy-crawly which clambered into bed with me from the dark. When I awoke the next day at dawn, the planet was in halcyon spirits, and I wondered if summer had somehow gone. The air temperature was cool, and atmosphere refreshingly clear after *the long night of blowing sand. I stepped out of my tent into pale light beneath a still ebony sky. The stars were gone in anticipation of the dawn. Day and night hung then in perfect balance. My fear of the desert was gone then too. I even contemplated the one-mile hike to The Edge of Deep-Water.*

The desert had me fooled. Not deliberately of course. There's far too much indifference here to support any malice. I was fooled by circumstance, and the natural confluence of events, and the quality and character of that particular morning's climate, and my own foolish trust of a clockwork universe of ever descending consequence.

I was slow to break camp then. I lured myself to complicit peace, and a quiet and settled attitude.

Suddenly the heat returned with force. It was about thirty minutes after those beams first touched my skin after sunlight spilled over the Bristol Mountains. I felt my internal temperature begin to rise, rising faster than sweat could control. Besides, I was thoroughly dehydrated from the dry night wind. There wasn't enough moisture in me to mount an effective thermal defense. I was losing the battle even before it really began. A little panic then. A little haste.

I broke camp quickly, and was on my motorcycle and moving along Route 66 in no time. That felt good. I was keeping the rising desert heat at bay through the wind of my ride, and the false sense of safety that our contraptions sometimes provide.

I stopped the bike once to admire a distant bajada. And another time to cast a melancholy gaze at the nothing that was once the ghost town of Bagdad. Neither time did I get off the bike. Neither time did I stop the engine. Two much risk in either action. Just keep moving. Forget about the heat.

About ten miles from my camp at Siberia I saw the low, black profile of the volcanic cinder cone called Amboy Crater, and my route began taking me past the crater's miles of hardened black lava. This is a particularly hot place, hotter than the surrounding desert. This is due to the black rocks which absorb heat to such an extent that you cannot touch them with bare skin, and which radiate this heat all day and night in great waves upon the land. This area is one of the origin places for the great winds which drive the sandstorms here, an origin place for many indifferent desert things.

On a whim I decided to pull into Amboy Crater at the Bureau of Land Management's narrow, one-lane paved road leading into the National Monument. I knew there were covered picnic tables by the trail head, which is the start of the two-mile walk to the crater summit. I thought I'd rest a bit in the shade. Ready myself for the long, two-hundred-mile ride home to the coast.

I woke an hour later to utter silence. The same midsummer daytime silence which speaks such volumes in the desert. There was nobody around when I'd arrived. Nobody came while I lay nearly naked on the concrete in the shade, ants climbing over my body, displaying the same open indifference I know so well here.

I sat up and rubbed my eyes, which squinted bloodshot and red, still stinging from the night's blowing sand. "Why do I do this?" I asked myself. "Why do I come to such places?" No answer was needed. The silence was answer enough. I didn't think anything more. Though I did write a short bit of prose then. I've copied it below. It's about the heat...and the cold. The twin killers as I called them. Here's what I wrote:

"There's an invisible killer prowling the entirety of the desert on a schedule both predictable and unposted. It swallows

202

everyone and everything at once, and begins squeezing until we're either dead, or it's time for departure has come. It will come again tomorrow, a little sooner or later depending on the season. It disappears for some months while its less dangerous fraternal twin takes its station. There's a short season of overlap when both twins can be met on the same day; though never at the same hour. Remember that these killers cannot be seen. Are soundless. Have no mind. And are utterly without mercy."

Six hours later I was home. Safe with my wife and daughter. Enjoying a long, cool swim in the pool.

Twenty-four hours after I left Amboy Crater, a husband and wife from Los Angeles drove into the same empty parking lot. I'm sure nobody else was there. They probably parked their car in the same spot where I'd parked my motorcycle, which was the most convenient location in the lot, close to both the shelter of the covered picnic benches and the trailhead. At around 11:00 AM the couple set out for the crater. By 2:00 PM both were dead.

~

One reason few people remain in the desert very long is the dawning awareness that arises here, that no legacy or memory can stay intact in such a hostile and dangerous place. Everything dies in the desert. Everything fades to dust and sand. Nothing remains or returns like it was before.

Elsewhere, in more mild climes, the fact of our growing and extending circles of family and friends, and the seeming permanence of what we've made or done in our lives, lead us to believe that the results of our life efforts will last, and maybe even survive for a while beyond our own passing. We imagine our life's work will stand for a time as a humble monument to our brief existence here. We're comforted we won't soon be forgotten. That after death, our name won't quickly become disconnect from the individual we once were. That anonymity will not sweep over us as it does every man, and every woman, and every child, who was, and who no longer is. That we won't at last become nothing more than a fading name, scratched, along with some dates, onto cut stone in a graveyard of forgotten someones. Old age and death are less fearful then, as we've fooled ourselves that our works will last for a while upon the earth, while our spirit will then go on to exist forever in heaven or hell. Such a curious equanimity. Such a deceitful peace.

Deserts offer no such peace. Deserts remind us that we are sand, and wind, and heat. Animated for a while. Alive for just another day. They inform us we have no soul. They tell us that death is no more than a return to the nothing we were so long before life. And deserts say these things without words. Speaking facts through mute and stark example. Caring not if we listen or comprehend. Incapable of caring even. Emptiness their first and final word.

This is why few who come remain long in the desert. This is why we come and then so quickly go. There's only so much we can take of such a place. Only so much we can stand, before we run back to our loved ones. Return to those who share our myths, and stories, and tales, and promise of comfort, permanence, and peace. To tell ourselves that what we began to suspect out in the desert isn't really true. To hold our hands to our ears and close our eyes. To speak reassuring words of forever. To talk of final reunion, and final reconciliation, and final justice. To speak again of forever, and then again. To talk of someday mansions in the clouds, and a just lawgiver who will love us forever. And of joy to last for eternity.

*We leave the desert to escape the denial of such comfort. We
leave the desert to forget the sand. To forget the silence. And
the heat. And the empty. And the utter indifference of a
universe that truly does not seem to care. And the awesome
implication these discovered facts suggest may be true.*

~

*The peaceful corridors of the mind. I'll walk there now and
again later. From time to time. So quiet. More silent even than
the desert at night. Not even the sound of crickets.*

~

*Tonight, will be the first evening in Siberia this summer when
the temperature at sunset will already be below 100 degrees (38
C.). I want to be there then. I want to walk alone towards the
darkening desert mountains then. I want to watch while the
killer makes its evening retreat to the east.*

*I haven't yet made a long nighttime excursion and overnight
into the deep water near my ghost town home of Siberia. My
reason is the fearful summertime heat which returns so soon
after sunrise, and my knowing reluctance to wake in the
morning far from the feign safety of my motorcycle, and the
necessity of hiking so far back while the Desert Killer begins
stalking in from the east. Twice in the past, the killer nearly got
me: once two years back, another time three decades before
that, when I was young, strong, and a very real danger to
myself.*

*The last time the desert almost caught me I had foolishly
lingered too long in the vicinity of deep water, and was nearly
taken as I attempted a hasty, and somewhat panicked escape
across and over a barren badlands of slippery, decomposed*

205

granite. As I jogged along and through the craggy rolling landscape, I worried that the loose rock would twist an ankle and leave me crippled and exposed to the coming killer. That experience was foolish, and the fear that I felt then was very real and well earned. I almost think I spotted death moving towards me then rather near from the north, from the deep end of the desert sea, wavering and flickering in the dry heat haze, a terrible mirage caught up in my panicked breathing, drawn to my hot, pounding pulse.

Before that—many decades before—I'd left my little red truck by the road on a late summer morning in the Panamint Valley. Without water, or a hat, or any protection at all, I'd decided to hike to a distant sand dune. So far, yet apparently so near. I turned back too late. Perhaps twenty minutes too late, having failed my goal. I was very frustrated, and so very stupid. I was nearly dead when I reached my truck again. My face was ghastly red. My body in the full riot of heat stroke. I later estimated I had probably less than thirty minutes of life left in me then. The killer had been directly on my heels, though I had no way to know him at that young age. I was then quite blind and immortal. It took several hours for my strong, healthy body to recover that day. It's been decades since, and my mind has still not overcome the experience.

Now I'm like a boy stung badly by bees who can't help returning to the hive. I gaze at the desert from a distance. I venture close when I can. I walk towards deep water where the threat is real. I always turn back before the killer spots me. I know I'm playing chicken with a force which will not flinch. I cannot let myself meet the killer again. I can't afford even to get close. I've far too much joy in life to risk fruitless death. I have proud responsibilities I both recognize and gladly own. I have my people and loved ones who count on me. And I have these strange words I do dearly love to write and share.

206

Yet I will go out again to tempt the killer. I'll watch it move across the desert at dawn, to storm and rage all day, and then pass away as the sun goes down. I'll watch. But I will not tempt. And I'll remember always that the killer will never know me. Even if it sees me. Even if it kills me. Even if I someday blunder and stumble into its path. It will never, ever know me.

~

It's interesting to note how the fearful things of my ordinary life refuse to accompany or follow me into the desert. Worries about money, career, or reputation drop away as I ride my motorcycle into the wastes. It's as though these things can find no purchase or footing in a place where their concerns have no relevance. Or perhaps it's simply because these worries become mean and petty in the face of the more real and permanent truths I encounter in their stead. Like the rich man who spills coins from his hands when he looks up to find the executioner at the door. Or the businessman who abandons all and runs ahead of an approaching plague. Or the well-known figure who chooses loved ones over adulation while lying upon his death bed. The curious thing is the way this effect lingers after my return. How I can walk like Caesar for days among my petty, civilized fears; looking down my nose at vanity, propriety, and esteem; respecting only love, and goodness, and virtue. I return always from the desert haunted and empowered by a grave truth I can only know by going deeper and further than I'd like, by going past the limit of the more common sense, by rejecting my base mortal fear, and by always going alone.

~

There are several ways to become lost in a desert. Only the most fortunate are never found. Even if they return to community, home, and loved ones, they are never found. Even

207

if they live long, and to a ripe old age, they are never found. Even if a subtle smile graces their countenance for the rest of their days, they are never found. Their blessing is being never found. Their great secret is being lost. Their humble wisdom is knowing no way back.

~

The following words are a confession of my selfish past and present, as well as a statement of my on-going effort at improvement. I note these things for the benefit of my daughter and her children should they somehow inherit my want of going alone.

I'd be lying if I said my path isn't scary. It is. The "going alone" theme isn't hyperbole. It's the perfect signpost on the faint trail where I prefer to walk, and the name of a destination I'll never reach. However, this route isn't nearly as solitary as it once was, as there are now some improved oases of human connection along the way, some better opportunity for time apart from the nowhere road to no place special.

I'm no longer as alone as I once was. I've my wife, and my daughter, and my brother, and my mom. Granted, I've always had these, though now I have them better than ever. And they have me. For better or for worse, we've each other now, and more than ever before.

Sadly though, the rest have fallen away. Or rather, I've let them all go. It's a rather mean and callus thing, to be sure. But so too would be the artificial maintenance of connections I no longer want, or need, or desire to keep. I suspect that if I'm not capable of being a very good friend, then it's probably best to not be one at all.

I do enjoy this quiet life. My strong, abiding preference has always been to be alone. I prefer the solitary company of my steps and my thoughts. I prefer the empty landscapes and long solitude of nights and days without others. I appreciate having no one to console or reassure me when I'm afraid of what's true. And I desperately want no one to distract me from the awful indifference which looms now across the horizon of my mind, and gapes like a cold void at the frontier of my every solitary adventure.

I'm lucky to have my wife. Thirty years together and she knows my journey. I've a partner who both allows and encourages this path I'm on. In the past, this going alone route sometimes drew me far away from her. Those were lonely times for us both. For me, the fact of being someone who was lost. For her, the fact of being married to someone lost, and the consequence of married solitude.

The last decade saw gradual improvement through the natural process of hard-won maturity, and the persistence of commitment to the values my wife and I both share, and which we attempt to instill in our daughter through both lesson and example. The key change was our fourteen months apart. That time when I came to America first, and left my wife and daughter behind in Japan. That experience broke me. Thankfully, I was broken then. After we were reunited, I was a new man. I understood better the value of my human contacts, especially my family. I gave up going alone then. And for two years I focused on becoming a better husband and father. A better man. I think I succeeded. The improved quality of our lives is testament to this change, as well as the patience of my family in waiting for me to catch up to values they already knew.

209

But I knew I hadn't really changed. I just knew better what was most important. I know that I can never fully get off the path of going alone. And with this realization I gave up my friends. I gave up my connections. I abandoned social media, and email, and reduced my online footprint to a single blog and an occasional video. I found a good balance. A disconnected balance. Disconnected from all but my most intimate connections. My wife, my daughter, my brother, and my mom.

Now I go alone again. Every two weeks on a Friday. I literally go alone then. I go off to the desert and disconnect for a full 24 hours. I then return and reconnect. I reconnect with my wife. And my daughter. And my brother. And my mom. There's little to no connection with anyone else.

My wife and I talk about this sometimes. She smiles and tells me she's lost her interest in other connections too. Perhaps this is a factor of our shared age. Or maybe it's because, though we are very different, we've nevertheless shared the same road together for most of our lives.

My wife and I spend far more and better time together now. We often smile at one another and hold hands like when we were dating, and we go places together, and we walk, and we talk, and we laugh like we once did. We just want each other now. And our daughter. And our brothers and sister. And our mother and father. And our little dog. And our little home. Our safe little corner of the universe. It's a place where The Great Indifference can only peek in through the window from the cold and dark outside, that is, if it had any interest, or ability, to do so. It has no place here now. Its place is out there, where nothing cares.

I sometimes look out our window on a peaceful and happy Sunday night with my family. And I wonder at the dead indifference staking the night out there in the dark. The dead indifference which was never alive and never died.

Still, this path scares me. For though I'm not fully alone, I know that I am alone. I found The Great Indifference early in life. And now I'm so far along there's no chance of turning back. Though even if I could, I'd never turn back. For how can reason rightly turn away from what it knows is true?

This path brings me closer each day to a once distant horizon growing near. It's a place I neither fear nor want. I can't turn back. And though I can't turn back, I know the remaining journey is secure with the ones I love. Secure until the moment we pass away forever from one another. With no chance of final reunion, no chance of final reconciliation, and no chance of final justice, I must attend to these things in the here-and-now. I must recognize and stand up to my fears now. No more cowardly hiding from this life through my time in the wastes. No more cowardly hiding from the wastes through my fear of what was never there.

~

I'm looking north from the edge of the desert ghost town of Siberia. I'm standing at the edge of the Deep-Water Wilderness which extends into the horizon. At left is Black Mesa, a place I haven't yet reached. At center, is the heart of Deep-Water; an intimidating badlands and maze-like moonscape of decomposed granite flash flood channels and gullies. At right can be seen the distant and hazy silhouette of the Old Dad Mountains, and the much nearer unnamed black volcano I visited last winter where I discovered the remains of "Campo #1."

211

I so want to strike out now into this wilderness. It's a place where humans seemingly never go. At least not since the 19th century gold miners gave up and left. I'd go out there now if I didn't know the killer was already on its way and ready to meet me. Instead, I'll head back to my motorcycle now. I'll escape while I still can. Already the temperature has risen drastically since sunrise. Or maybe that's just my fear. Either way, it's a good time to get away.

~

My GSA motorcycle is packed and ready to go. It's a shame to leave though...just as my imagination and thinking were acclimating to the silence and solitude. But that's alright, as bits of this peace always follow me home, adding incrementally to the joy and meaning of a well-lived life.

~

In Japan, the landscapes I explored appeared new and young, almost adolescent. With steep and rugged mountains rising direct from the sea, and long, narrow valleys twisting into impossibly remote, mist covered peaks. Everywhere the rocks were jagged and angular, as though freshly fallen from cliffs and peaks. The mountains of Japan also roar and tinkle always with the sound of flowing water, unbelievable quantities of clean, fresh and cold water melting from snowy alps, percolating from saturated mountain soils, and raging through wild streams and rivers, which rise and swell with abundant rainfall and the torrent of seasonal typhoons. The landscape has the character of youth, being bold, brash, and full of life and abundant energy. I was always in awe of the wilderness in Japan, though the effect was somewhat superficial, like the experience of watching a skilled athlete in control of a young and powerful body, or the impetuous activities of youth, newly animated with

212

the spirit of discovering they are alive. These things are impressive, though not often moving.

The American desert is very different. My time alone in wild places here is like a stroll through a mausoleum of geology. The mountains are ancient and worn, the greater part of their being having been reduced to the sand beneath my feet. The rocks are angular like the rocks in Japan, though in the desert they stay this way for eons, there being little rain to capture, move and grind away their rough edges. The water that does come is powerful, yet brief and fleeting, like the smile of an old man remembering the joys of youth while the Reaper places its hand upon his shoulder. And the desert is quiet, and silent, and at peace. The desert always has my respect, and at times moves me like a great teacher or quiet sage, though I know it is neither.

I'm glad I've known both landscapes. I'm grateful for the character lesson of each, as well as the example of good living they provide through two quite distinct and different seasons of life.

~

I realize now that my repeated visits to Siberia have left an imprint there which I neither intended nor wanted. My brief living at that spot has marked it with my passage; and added something to the mystery of that place.

I always set up my camp at Siberia in the same spot. It's an area both convenient to my motorcycle, and slightly protected from the desert's prevailing east wind. The sand beneath where I place my tent has become soft due to my removal of all but the smallest stones. And the four corners where I pound my tent stakes are clearly marked with the large stones I use to secure

213

these into the ground. Finally, there's a small section of cut wooden railroad tie with a small metal grate secured to the top. This item is stuck into the sand just outside the rectangle of stones. I found this item in the desert some months back; and brought it to camp to serve as my cook table. This is my camp at the desert ghost town of Siberia. It's a rough place of stone, sand, wood, and steel. Yet it's origin of human hands is clear. It's an artifact of human caring.

The effect of these symmetrically placed stones, surrounding an area of fine sand, and accented with a wood and metal grate, suggests human intervention. It's the same thing I experience now when I encounter old graves in the desert, or when I first discovered that stone-lined footpath through the middle of Siberia. These things tell us someone's been here. They suggest someone once cared in a place where caring has long since departed.

My contribution to the mystery of Siberia is a rectangular perimeter of rock, surrounding a bed of soft sand, and an accent of wood and metal. I realize now that even if I never go back to Siberia, my fingerprints are there. My mark on that place is secure. I've added yet another strange human assembly of objects to that place. I've produced yet another mystery of stone and debris. Something to perhaps catch and puzzle the mind of anyone who visits and looks closely, today, tomorrow, or a hundred years from now.

~

The young man I once was would never join me in the desert. He'd know better than to not go alone. He'd make up some polite excuse to tell me no before giving me the social slip. I'd be proud of his foresight then, even if I knew he didn't understand the reason he must go alone.

214

My young self would be such a burden in the desert. So lost, and searching, and full of energy, questions, and pointless speculation. I'm glad I wasn't there when I was that young man.

I'd never invite my younger self to the desert with me. I'd do him that small favor at least. Otherwise, I'd be perfectly silent with him. I wouldn't tell him a single thing.

~

Just a hint of my return to the desert and my muse descends upon me as from nowhere. Is it really this easy to summon poetry, art, and the product of rich and fulfilling imagination? This strange catalyst of beauty, depth and meaning, always at hand, forever at the ready, at least as long as our faculty of mind persists, and our will to bend along the path of our natural inclination remains.

~

The desert is not a good place of escape, as the wide-open spaces provide nowhere to hide. There's no distance too far to separate us from what we deny or fear, which trails us easily in a landscape where the only footprints are our own. For the sake of hiding, it's much better to stay put within our safe and familiar, to bury ourselves under piles of routine, and cover our eyes with the ordinary. I fear the desert not for the risk of becoming lost, but instead for the very real threat of being found.

~

The forecast tonight for the East Mojave Desert is mild temperatures and high winds. The experience of shutting off the big motorcycle's engine after arriving in such a place, and

215

under such circumstances, is not unlike plunging headlong from rocks into a mild churning sea.

Switching off the motorcycle's engine then is a shock. After 200 miles of riding, the sudden quiet is deafening, like an implosive concussion drawn in by the sudden cessation of sound. Night, and deep darkness flood in as the bike's single headlight cuts out. Darkness and silence at once reign. The effect is enveloping, encapsulating, and smothering.

Immediately though, the wind pushes aside the silence, and the night. There's a particular sound the wind makes in the desert at night. It's a rustling sound, the sound of confusion, the sound of disorder, the sound entropy makes as it slowly fills the universe with waste.

At this moment I'll stand upon the desert sand with my legs apart, a firm stand against the wind, a resolute posture in the face of the night. A long night. Even after the daylight comes, a very long night.

~

I've arrived in the desert ghost town of Siberia. This place is more empty now than ever. There's no muse, no ghost, and no god. Even the wind is hush, and only whispers through the branches of the creosote brush. Curiously, there's no fear here either. Those phantoms were never real anyway. Though for most of my life I allowed them some say over my imagination and anxiety. No more now. There's nothing here but sand, stone, wind and quiet. Sure, there's mortality too. Nothing to fear there either. Only a deeper and more silent dark than even the desert can muster.

*It takes time for our mind to adjust to solitude in wild places.
To overcome our settled sense, and shrug off the norms and
conventions of social habit. I feel these things falling away
slowly with every step removed into the wild. The sense is like
becoming aware of a great apparatus and structure being
carried upon the back, which I only note as it begins to fall
away, piece by piece[8]. How many steps would be necessary to
remove it wholly? Is that even possible? What creature would I
then become?*

~

*The place I visited yesterday startled me for its natural artistry,
and seeming permanence in time, and will-less beauty. While
crossing over a rugged badlands of soft-colored pink and pale
granite, a place devoid of visible life save some specimens of
tiny red cactus blending easily with the stones and sand, I came
upon a flat high point displaying a curious natural feature called
desert pavement. This strange geologic phenomenon occurs in
deserts, and mainly in areas where steady winds blow over high
relief ground littered with tiny stones. The stones in this
particular spot came from a nearby outcrop of reddish volcanic
rhyolite peeking up through the much older granite country
rock. Millennia of alternating heat and cold had chipped to bits
the exposed face of hard rhyolite which were then scattered
evenly by random winds over an area roughly the size of a
tennis court. This spot was perched on a perfectly flat rise
overlooking a 360-degree landscape view encompassing
roughly two hundred square miles of empty desert. The wind
here was strong and steady, and probably had been day after
day, not for weeks or months, but for centuries and millennia.
The constant wind had the working effect of a stone mason
who might carefully arrange the broken rhyolite into a perfect*

217

mosaic before blowing away the sand. Working over many centuries with wind from different angles, and with the seeming accuracy of an Egyptian pyramid builder, the reddish puzzle pieces and pebbles had been blown about and fitted perfectly together with exacting accuracy. The final result was a perfectly flat expanse of desert stone, formed not as a solid sheet of rock, but instead as a fitted composite of tiny rocks perfectly placed by the hand of wind, and time, and chance, and an eternity of mindless patience. I sat upon the stones then to remove my shoes and walk barefoot (mindful of the small cactus) over the smooth face of natural art I'd found, perhaps never before seen by human eyes. I then sat for a long time upon the pavement and thought as the warm desert wind blew steady at my back. I thought of all the small haphazard events which had created this natural wonder, and of all the time it took to complete. I thought of the art of nature, which neither cares for recognition and praise, nor is capable of perceiving when such is offered. And I thought of my own brief witness of this same, and the hurried way even this small recognition and perception must soon be swept away like the sand which long ago was blown like waste from this desert rise.

~

I failed to reach the deep end of the desert this weekend despite the fact I hiked in further than I had in over a year. Depth clearly isn't a function of distance, though some distance is clearly needed.

~

I'm beginning to detect a subtle vacuum force within the desert which draws me away to places I've difficulty climbing back from. I've so far tempted this force with no more than a day's

218

journey, which I've always easily escaped. I'll soon try two days of depth. I wonder how much harder the climb back will be?

~

Last week's trip to Siberia was my first night arrival on the motorcycle. The ghost town is located in an enormous valley of roughly 200 square miles without another human being anywhere. The only sign of human life here are the long trains which pass by occasionally in the night, and the one or two cars which glide through the dark like phantoms along Route 66. The darkness here is utter and complete on moonless nights like this, and when I shut off the motorcycle's engine, and kill the light, the night swarms in like a smothering blanket, and I find myself gazing up at the stars like the hopeful companions they'll never be.

~

My reconnoiter last week to the edge of the Deep-Water Wilderness has revealed the Desert Killer is gone. This means I can plan my first extended desert hike since returning to the USA. I'm thinking a two-days, two nights, outing from Siberia, through Deep-Water and into the black mountains. I'd lie if I told you the thought of going so far alone doesn't scare me. Especially as I know my little god will certainly not join me there. I'm learning now there's good reason the deep desert is sometimes described as a forsaken land.

~

These last two trips to the desert were more alone than ever, which is the aim, and purpose of going. My companions in solitude were absent: the muse, the Desert Killer, my little god. Only indifference remained, which is devoid of

219

companionship, and the thing which fills the solitude with
empty.

~

It's a little difficult to describe how alone I felt out here this
night. There was literally no sign of humanity in any direction,
not even the lights of airplanes. Only the wind made any effort
at motion, or sound, or any activity which suggested I was still
within the world of animate movement or life. Though there
was no life here which would care for me—I'd left them a day
away, in another world, and a place I could barely muster to
memory for the fact of its very real distance of mind—I was
nevertheless very, very alone with the soulless beasts roaming
the dark, reminding me that I too have no soul, and therefore
no capacity to survive any darkness greater than this night. And
though I was alone, I knew that I was still not as alone as I'd yet
like to be. Going alone is a far and deep trespass into places we
both fear and marvel, and it is always possible to go too far, and
always a fact that we must each one day go further than we can
ever return. I'm not nearly ready to go that far. I've far too
much love of life to wish that feign passage anytime soon. So,
when the full moon finally began peeking over the invisible
Black Mountain to the east of my night camp at Deep-Water, I
knew I'd then enjoy some relief from the deep night, and some
rest from the delicious anxiety of deep solitude which ever has
the capacity to satisfy, while always leaving more emptiness than
was hoped for or sought.

~

It's still thirteen hours before I'll step away from my motorcycle
and plunge headlong into the desert night, to begin a two-hour
hike through darkness to The Edge of Deep-Water. Already
though, I sense the nothingness and empty of the deep desert

*come sniffing at my heels, seeking out my weakness, begging
me to remember my fear. This feeling will only grow through
the day; though it will dispel instantly once I'm swallowed by
the night.*

~

*Tonight's hike will begin at Siberia roughly an hour after
sundown. The moon will be nearly full, providing pale
illumination and rendering the landscape to shades of light gray
against the black canopy of space. If I keep my flashlight turned
off, then my eyes will adapt to the dark and I'll easily pick my
way through the desert, past obstacles such as rocks, cactus and
creosote brush, However, without my light, I might not spot
rattlesnakes which come out to hunt in the dark. With the light
on, my pupils will close, and my world will shrink to a shallow
pool of bright illumination guiding my footsteps through the
night. I'll then easily spot snakes, tarantula, and scorpions;
through without any trail to follow I'll need to rely on instinct,
and the position of the moon, as my guides. From time-to-time
I'll stop, turn off the light, and wait while my eyes readjust to
the dark, and I can pick out the silhouette of the low mountains
to the north which are my aim, and the edge of the Deep-
Water Wilderness.*

*After an hour or so of hiking through the dark, I should reach
the edge of the Bristol Mountains. I'll need to select, in the
dark, a narrow canyon to follow up, and into, the badlands,
which are my destination, and where I hope to reach before
setting up camp for the night. These canyons are narrow, with
many small, dry waterfalls. So, I'll need to hike carefully, and
remain extra vigilant for snakes which hunt for rodents among
the rocks. During daylight hours (when the snakes are hiding) I
often see their winding tracks in the sandy places between the
stones.*

An hour later I should be near my goal. After a tricky scramble up a steep slope of decomposed granite, I'll come upon the badlands mesa I call The Edge of Deep-Water. From here, when I turn off my light, I can see over two hundred square miles of empty desert, between the Bullion Mountains to the south, the Old Dad Mountains to the north, the Granite and Providence Mountains to the east and the extinct volcano of Pisgah (which name means "summit" in Hebrew; and was the mountain from whence God showed Moses the Promised Land) to the west. In all that vast space there will be only two signs of humanity, which are the twin red beacons atop the Bullion Mountains marking the site of remote radio towers.

In this place...I will stay the night.

~

I'd fooled myself into thinking the Desert Killer was gone. I'd mistaken the killer for summer heat, and deep winter cold, and imagined some respite now between the extreme seasons. But I sensed it now as I rode my motorcycle down into the desert, and away from the living comfort of my species. I sensed the killer out there in the dark, floating amidst the blind hills and mute mountains, over a landscape illuminated with faint moonlight; a natural light illuminating the indifference and the grave things we all strive to forget over the course of our lives, until these things emerge from the fearful wastes to find us. I have no more need to fear the desert night than the warm and happy nest my family and I call home. The Desert Killer can find us now in either place, only out here I can better see it coming.

~

Such fear just before my arrival at Siberia. Terror of a sort, really. The fear hit me about a mile out, while slowing the bike to spot the dirt road where I turn off Route 66. I'm always scared at this point. But tonight...wow! That little coward within let out a yelp and a squawk saying "GOOO! Don't turn! Just go back the way you came!" Of course, I ignored him. I nearly always do. He's always wrong. Though I suspect one day he'll be right.

~

The waitress at Barstow kindly filled my thermos with hot coffee, so I'll have a cup here at Siberia before I start out walking into the mountains. The moonlight is superb! And I can see the black hulks of the Bristol Mountains a few miles off to the north. The darkness within the mountains seems another thing, though I know I'll be able to see fine once I get there. The fear should pass shortly. It's interesting how cowardice so quickly flies before resolve.

~

I'm back. The wilderness definitely got the best of me this time. I feel like a boxer who's gone several rounds with an opponent way outta his league. The feeling is good though, as it's satisfying to press limits and explore weakness of both body and mind. I'm sure I'll be thinking about the last 48 hours for years to come. I'm glad I have the chance to do these things while I still can. However, it's a bit unsettling to discover my body is now more fit for the wild than my mind.

I found a note left for me on my motorcycle at the ghost town of Siberia, left for me by a young railroad signalman who I'd met over the summer when he stopped by Siberia to maintain the railroad signal there. I left a note for him in return, as well as a nice specimen of million-year-old petrified wood from the surrounding mountains.

~

The fear I experienced this week in the desert has been on my mind. It was that second night, or better, the two hours leading up to sundown, which really pushed my limits. I was well into the Deep-Water Wilderness, further than I'd ever gone. I'd left my gear on the ground an hour back, in the shadow of a large stone cliff. I thought I could go further and faster with just the bare essentials. I didn't even bring water, which was already running short, choosing to trade thirst for speed, which I deemed equitable given the way the desert was cooling as the sun dipped nearer the horizon. After an hour of up and down, left and right, across an exposed landscape of silence and wind—silence in the low hollows, and wind upon the relief—I made a hard scramble up a slippery granite slope to a summit capped with a crown of jagged rock, like teeth growing from the land. The wind was howling here, and cold, as through premonition of the coming night's deep chill. That wind; the way it blew past my ears; as though reminding me of my mortality; telling me how frail and vulnerable I was. This was my own mind speaking of course. The wind didn't care. The cold was senseless to my presence; and the coming night would envelope the land with or without my approbation. Placing a hand upon the jagged summit, I looked out over the land before me, and shivered more deeply than the cold would warrant. A cliff in front of me dropped sharp into a deep

224

canyon of many colors, a place which would seem beautiful at any other time, but which now appeared terrifying for the fact that I would not want to be down there. To go there would be to enter both silence and cold, as the shadows of night had already arrived down there, and the long deepening of night, and the onset of cold, were well underway. I looked beyond the dark canyon to a maze of narrow, twisting valleys, steep cliffs, and jagged peaks—darkness everywhere below me. I wanted nothing to do with that place; not then at least; not under those circumstances. I turned and made my way quickly back to where I'd left my gear, to the relief of water, and the warmth of a jacket, and the relative security of my few familiar things. Yet the darkness of that canyon followed me back, enveloping me as I set up camp, and then smothering me with utter night after the sun was gone, moving away only after the full moon rose in the east an hour after sundown. Yet by then I knew the darkness and the moonlight were really one, brothers in a way. Only our human love of beauty and poetry ascribe loveliness and comfort to the one, and fear and solitude to the other. They are, in truth, equally indifferent. The darkness and moonlight hiding or illuminating equally well a breathing man as well as a corpse, having neither capacity nor faculty to care in any case. It's these times when I think deeply of my loved ones, when I remember their voices, and their faces, and the lives we live and share. Those thoughts keep back the night, assuage the fear, and fool my mind into forgetting, for a moment, the indifference is really there.

~

Coming upon the deserted mining site of Campo #1. This place is exceedingly quiet. When the wind is still, the only sound is a slight, rhythmic thumping which appears to be coming from within. In fact, the sound is from within, and is the noise blood cells in the eardrum make as they bang into

225

one another flowing through the body. I've only ever heard this sound in very remote places deep within the desert. And most clearly when going alone.

~

There's something perfect about hiking at night. But only if there's no trail to follow, and no companion to share the way. For how else can the mind better become lost, with no signpost or path to guide and constrain our step? How much easier to perceive the soulless beasts which prowl the night, and know that we are their kin, than if we forgo our own kinship with a species which pretends we are more? I'd walk all night alone into deepening dark places if only my will and courage were the equal to my desire to face what is true.

~

I first became aware of the soulless beasts when I began hiking alone at night in the desert. I'd encounter these beasts suddenly, as a fox in my path, or a snake along the sand, or a large wandering spider crawling over my shoe. Even the energetic moths which assault my flashlight give out an air of mechanical disinterest, of purpose driven of instinct and lust, hunger, or unthinking determination. I began to call these creatures "soulless beasts" as a means to describe their seeming familiarity and comfort with the pervasive indifference of the desert night, not realizing my implicit bias that I was somehow different. Yet the soulless beasts know better. Though they don't care for me, they do remind me with their caution, fear, and their own keen indifference that I too am one of them. The full mortality which glistens in their eyes reflects my own distant fear of death. The beasts stare at me and through me at once, my life of neither interest nor consequence to them beyond their own primitive needs. I tell myself that my interests

226

are something more; that my ends of a greater aim. The beasts though are unconvinced, as too the dark desert night. Even the wind rustles ignorance, which is no more than a frail cover for indifference. I'm convinced at last that I too am a beast. And I walk on into the night. After first switching off the light.

~

Though I know I've no real reason to be afraid, I'll confess to some anxiety tonight when I realized that "Campo #1" may be the place I once referred to as "the woodsman's cabin on the near side of Mt. Wildness." It's a frightful thing when fiction becomes reality, and the haunted places of the mind refuse to stay with the imagination.

~

The wilderness absorbs my life energy like sunlight into beach sand; warming the landscape slightly, minutely animating the passage of time. My wanderings, thoughts, and ambitions dissolve away to nothing with each aimless footstep. Purpose here has as much value as a diamond lost in the sand. Memory as much reach as the mortal who remembers. Solitude is the key to this grim vista. Walk with another to hide the way. Close your eyes to pretend the indifference isn't.

~

My book needs a chapter on death; though this theme already pervades every section and page. Is it enough to reflect the atmosphere of indifference with my words? Should I also make explicit effort to relate what I've found haunting the wastes, and also the places where my species makes noise and laughter to push away the night? Perhaps it's enough to let the finality beyond life blow like the cold desert wind; or sit for millennia

227

*like a desert rock slowly turning to sand. I should then simply
allow these things to be. Let the wind blow, and the Earth turn
to sand. Let the story be told to both the day and the night, the
living, and the dead, and most clearly to whoever will go alone.*

~

*This was a long and distant hike. Further perhaps than
necessary. Though it's telling that next time I'll go further. It's
those black mountains to the north which are my destination.
Two nights out should do the job, as long as I've the internal
fortitude and courage to leave it all behind and push hard past
the place my mind keeps telling me to turn back. It's such a
primitive and fearful thing this little mind of mine. So afraid of
what isn't real, and what it doesn't know, and the things which
once rightfully frightened the timid creatures we all once were.*

~

*I'm a hundred miles out from Siberia, enjoying a last supper of
sorts at the Denny's restaurant in Barstow. When I arrive at the
ghost town two hours from now, I'll leave the motorcycle with
the ruins, and head out into the dark desert for a long two or
three-hour night hike to the trackless Deep-Water Wilderness.
After crossing several miles of sloping alluvium, I'll climb up
and onto a dark, flat mesa of volcanic rhyolite, which is The
Edge of Deep-Water, and the place where I stayed and slept
the last time I was here alone after dark; a place where my fear
was assuaged with the sound and sight of distant freight trains
passing through the black empty desert far below, reminding
me that I wasn't then truly alone, wasn't yet completely
disconnected from my kin and kind. This ancient fear and
comfort—a curious pair and juxtaposition—which kept me
company the last time at this place, is the thing I hope to push
past tonight by continuing on further from the mesa, down off*

228

*the dark height, into the still darker depths of true deep water;
to walk on further, 'till the trains grow silent, and the tendrils of
comfort snap and disappear for their insignificant bonds. I'll
walk on then through the night to the place where the soulless
beasts live, to join their number, to walk in their example, to
remember what I really was, am and must at last one day
become.*

~

*A soulless beast came snuffling around my tent last night. It was
well past midnight; a long time asleep; too much sleep. I'd gone
to bed early, as I'd no campfire to comfort or keep back the
night. Too much sleep indeed. I wasn't as deeply gone as I
should have been...when I heard a gentle tapping against the
flap of my tent. Not a tapping really, so much as a sliding
sound, as if some blunt paw were being passed over the fabric.
It was the lighter, softer version of the sound a dog makes when
it paws the door to be let it. A gentle night wind was blowing,
true. But the wind sounds are distinct, with a mindless, random
cadence, hinting at inanimate origins and an utter lack of intent.
This other sound wasn't random—nor was it without purpose.
This other sound was the product of a mind—a soulless mind,
like my own.*

*I heard it once—three or four gentle rasps—which brought me
out from my slight slumber. And then—carefully listening—I
heard it again, close at hand by my right ear, which was nearest
the tent's edge. Did the soulless thing outside in the dark sense
my position within the tent? Had it come near my ear to ensure
it was heard? Only inches away, separated by a thin veil of
fabric? I hovered between fear, and curiosity and wonder. I
thought of my geology hammer by my side, imagining a sudden
battle between myself and the thing outside. Such a wasted
thought. Such a poor use of time. I'd come all this way, so far
alone into the wild, to imagine a fight with the unknown?*

229

Couldn't I do better with this time? Make improved use of the fact of the thing outside my tent?

I listened for a while before drifting back to sleep. There were no more sounds then. Though later, a few hours before dawn, after the moon had set, and all darkness ruled, I thought I heard something paw past in the dark; something defiant of the night, and the bitter cold; defiant even of me, the master of the planet, come to the wild to stand and walk like an immortal. I think it's the fact that I've no soul—and that I know it—which gives the beasts their ease in questioning my presence; and trespassing my camp; and denying any vain wish or hope that the cold and empty night...are not.

~

The ruins at Campo #1 are in no way improved by my presence. The human dream and want of that place vanished long ago. It is now more wild than if my species had never come. My visits provoke more melancholy longing than warmth. There's more empty here than the wildness beyond the camp. Ruins have this effect. It's the same feeling we know when we touch and handle a memento of a loved one who has passed. A cold warmth of remembrance of something forever lost.

~

Unoccupied rooms can acquire the quality of empty desert; not in fact, but in terms of human neglect and disregard, like a toy where there are no children, or a companion without company. Though the character of these are the same, the desert has a much deeper reserve of empty. Walking alone in the deep desert is like swimming where water depth is measured in miles rather than meters. Our feet twist and kick above a deep chasm we cannot cross alive, nor know in death. It's an impossible

230

gap; where the gentle swell of the sea lifts us now and again to glimpse another impossible reach across to the horizon, and still another over our heads into space.

When we enter a long empty room, or handle a forgotten toy, or meet our want of others where none can be found; we know for a few moments that same aching empty found strong and hard in the wild; and while the effect is weak among civilized things, dissipating fast before our touch and gaze, the empty is not so easily moved where humans fail to go. It remains like reality against the force of imagination. I would beat my hands against this fact were it my folly to believe there were something more.

~

Almost ten years ago I invented the fiction of Mt. Wildness; a place in my mind which typified the remote wilderness of deep Japan. I never found Mt. Wildness there, though I sometimes heard the howling from that place, and I knew the approximate location of the long-deserted woodsman's cabin on the near side of the mountain.

When I came to America, I forgot about Mt. Wildness for a time; focused instead on more practical aims, necessities which denied much leisure in imaginary places.

Those necessities are now handled; and lately, during my routine outings to the wild, I've heard what sounds like the howling on Mt. Wildness. This couldn't be... That place can't be here. Mt. Wildness was a fiction for Japan; nowhere else.

I even began calling an impostor peak within The Deep-Water Wilderness, Mt. Wildness—though I knew this wasn't true.

231

Today though, I've found it... It was during lunch; and while scanning satellite imagery of the desert beyond The Sandman's Bed; a place impossibly far—as Mt. Wildness must be—at the end of a trackless path, in a place where none are welcome.

Now I need to scheme a way to get there—alone of course, so as to not scare away what isn't real.

~

Ghost town cemeteries are sufficient reminder that there are no ghosts, nor even memories, when there is no one left to remember.

~

I'm starting to get at, and uncover, the haunting thing which I always meet while alone in the deep wild. When it finds me— usually at night—I have to swallow hard to get down the animal fear and instinct of a million years. Our fearful programming is no childish thing, as the danger of our mortality is real; though circumstance and fact are not what they used to be. Instead of fangs and claws, my worry now is the smallness of my flickering light, which gutters and bends in the winds of midlife. We forget this fact while at home and at work, where the company and nearness of others cause the impression that our individual lights are somehow pooled; made brighter through an aggregate sense of society. We believe then that our light is more likely to sustain should one or the other of us go out. There's truth to this, at the indifferent level of heredity and genes, though it's false to think our flame will truly go on, as death does seemingly do irrevocable harm and ruin to every life which will ever live. All alone then in the wild, with the darkness of the universe crowding close, our little flame consumes hungrily at what small fuel we are. There's no reassuring comfort here of others; no warm and friendly flames of friends and loved ones

232

*to offer false hope; only the cold light of the soulless beasts
moving indistinctly out there in the deep night, looking upon
our little light as nothing more than another silent and pale
twinkle in the coming empty.*

~

*The place outside the pale of human light, or life even, draws
pain in those unfamiliar with such wastes. It's why such subjects
are taboo to speak of, or masked in myth and superstition. Yet
the dead acknowledge these facts, as much the granite stone or
the cold light of distant stars. At what point must the living
confess mortality's incessant demand of truth? At the point of
shut down, when disease or old age rob us of our motivation to
lie, and our tongues cease motion, while our eyes gaze far, and
our loved ones look on, wondering where we've gone, before
we're really gone.*

~

*Don't go alone in the wild unless you're willing to learn just
how far diminishing returns can really go.*

~

*The great beasts of the California desert are the mile-long
freight trains which lumber along the empty; bearing relevance
through a land which couldn't care less. These trains are great
and powerful and awe-inspiring—especially at night, and at close
quarters, when the moon is new, and the nighttime utter, and
the depth of darkness penetrates further than we'd like. I
sometimes sit up in the night to watch these long trains passing.
They remind me of my kind, and my people, and the
community and society we hold in common. These things
matter much less out here in the night after the trains have*

passed, and the night resumes its deteriorating ways, and darkness peeks still closer where we'd rather it never shine.

~

Sometimes when I'm alone, and very far into wilderness, I look back and realize suddenly that I've been swallowed by the empty. It's the understanding that there's as much wildness behind me, as there is in front of me, and again on every side, that triggers the panic. When the fear comes, I usually start talking out loud to no one way out there in the nowhere. It's a strange dialogue between the part of me that is freaking out, and another side which is calmly talking away the fear, with a plan and the force of reason. When I was younger, the panic often won, and I'd sometimes literally run from the place which brought on the fear. This hasn't happened though in years, and I usually now simply sit myself down to wait out the irrational fear. The fear always fades. The quiet and peace—and peace of mind—always return.

Anchorhold

The place where we suffer and die

STOIC POETRY

Recognizing the scope of our control

*"It takes a tranquil and untroubled mind
to roam freely across all parts of life."*

-Seneca

I owe much to ancient Greek and Roman Stoic thinkers and the influence they have had on Western culture and society. I suspect my hero, Henry David Thoreau, was influenced directly, or indirectly, by Stoic writing, as he often refers to values proposed and supported by Stoic thinkers, such as Marcus Aurelius, Epictetus, and Seneca. If I could have my youth to do over again, I would include in my late teens the writings of these men, which I did not otherwise discover until midlife. So influenced, I suspect I could have avoided much of the struggle and hardship of life reconciliation during the decades of my twenties, thirties, and forties, which otherwise required many hard knocks to liberate some sense into my living. This section of my book is dedicated to words which I knowingly wrote with the Stoics in mind. This section is my homage to the Stoic perspective and way of life, which has done much to refine my sensibilities, and without which I could not have composed my Good Life plan of living at this late stage of my life. Or perhaps ever.

Notes from my muse

I told a man my mind and he asked me "What efforts have you made to destroy this idea? And how may I help to bring it

down?" What a worthy friend. So caring of my best interest.
Let us war together upon my claims to truth.

~

Create a garden within your mind. A place hemmed in by
reason. Where you can nurture virtue in true soil. A quiet and
simple sanctuary, ever present, always home.

~

Virtue is independent of possessions. Though what we have or
want may distract us from virtue.

~

What is it you can truly touch? Even your raised voice will only
carry so far. Distinguish these things. Measure your reach.
Attend to practical ends.

~

What small routines, mindful actions, and discerning ways
reveal the wilderness passage.

~

Shout your musings down the corridors of time
They echo and return
Lost at last

~

Virtue rests in tempered self-reflection. Not much. Just enough to gather the facts. Just enough to gain accurate perspective for the application of reason. Let it go then. And think not of events other than your rational conclusions and the resolutions they entail. And never gawk or dwell upon the circumstance of others, which is an intemperate indulgence, and a distraction from your own true labor. Attend the mending of your own folly, which you alone can repair. And burden not your neighbor with any prying misattentions.

~

The routines and vain actions of life are but a bluff and distraction from living. Bright and shiny. New and interesting. Our lives given over to awe and wonder. Our better purpose is ignored. The considered life. The principled life. A life of discipline and temperance. A life spent enacting and enforcing the laws we must ourselves discover and ratify. Police, barrister, judge and perhaps executioner. Engaged in the messy business of applying reason to our base animal thoughts, in the hope of forming something true from instinct, emotion and gasping higher thought. Gasping like a man drowning in the sea of evolved conclusions. And when that higher mind sputters some words of good sense above the waves, how then to remember and live in accord with what we've found? When all the sea rages, and none may hear our voice over the froth and din. Still we go on. Swimming towards something better. Straining muscle with willful, disciplined strokes. Until we at last drown, and sink again below the mad waves. Attaining nothing more than the best life we knew how. That's the thing we seemingly seek to avoid.

~

Let every act of virtue be self-contained
At once thought, action and reward
Seeking nothing more
And asking no notice or remembrance

~

Do I die now in equanimity?
Then I've indeed reached a good end.

~

This balanced and tuned apparatus
So frail and fleeting
Upon which my everything is carried
Through places and years
Always now...
So near nevermore

~

Be responsible for what is within your control. Let others own
their own thoughts and flesh.

~

My first thought at every challenge: What opportunity this
moment virtue?

~

Humbly acquiesce to sound principle

~

How might I bear well this worthy burden
Carry this necessary weight
Tolerate painful right action
Rather than flee to easy salvation

~

When challenge arrives
And panic rises in the heart
Still then the mind
Still more the tongue

~

These few square meters of flesh are far more than I can
maintain or cultivate. Ruin progresses despite plan and action.
My only real estate is my will. A moment-by-moment
application of hard-earned best practice. Applied to the ends
revealed of reason.

~

I'd rather take less, or give up my portion, than suffer the loss
of nourishing restraint.

~

My response is all I really own. The rest are like leaves blown
in an autumn wind.

~

It's easy to become a monster
Simply follow
When you know you should lead
Your spirit will die
And something hollow...
And rotten
Will fill the empty space

~

Man, and womanhood are sufficient ends
To a stout and earnest mind
Dismissive of distraction
Heedless of precedent
Careless of legacy...
Fearless of death
Consumed of resolve
To speak one true thing
To fill the empty space

~

Peace is easy
When expectation is reduced
To the level of reality

~

To give more
And want less

~

*Let not a single thought escape my mind which has not
suffered the scrutiny of reason.*

~

*The sober subject of our lives' decline arrives so often late to
the feast, and long before the diner has enjoyed their fill.*

~

*Would you detain or lament Death's rightful trespass; throw up
protest and complain perceived misfortune; cry like a child
denied sovereignty over all they see and know? To what
end...that your gravity and equanimity might go first before the
gallows?*

You've made it...
there and back

At least on paper

You've perhaps come a long way,
Without me

Now, I have just a little more to say,
Before we part ways

I'll summarize now,
What came of my own adventure,
What I made of the journey,
And how I made a *good life*,
Of what I didn't find

THE GOOD LIFE

Creating a life of meaning

"He could not bear the indifference of life any longer, could not endure being cast off and thrown back on himself again and again. No home on earth, no God in heaven, no goal out there in the future! He would at least have a home. He would make it his own by loving everything there, big and little, every rock, every tree, the animate and the inanimate; he would portion out his heart to it all so that it could never cast him off again."

-Jens Peter Jacobsen

The Good Life Meditation is my daily effort of recounting, considering, and developing my personal life objectives and principles. I perform this activity in the morning, usually on my way to work, as a start and readiness to the coming day, and as a reminder of the best life practices I have so far uncovered and made my own. With practice, the effort has become as familiar and refreshing as making and enjoying a hot cup of coffee, leaving me fortified and invigorated for whatever the day may hold.

Note: I periodically record this activity on video to upload to a special YouTube playlist titled "The Good Life." I recommend watching one of these videos for more in-depth coverage of each point, as well as personal examples of how I apply these objectives and principles to my own daily challenges. The playlist URL is included in the appendix[9].

Affirmation of human and civil rights

I must recognize, respect, and abide the rights of individuals and the smaller groups within society such that these are not compromised in the pursuit of the common good.

Eight objectives

1. **BE ALWAYS READY TO DIE,**
   or become infirm, or old

   "That we must all die, we always knew; I wish I had sooner remembered it."

   -Dr. Johnson

   At all times, have every important life affair in order: my decided purpose, my household, and finances, as well as my connections, obligations, responsibilities, and commitments. Have also my art in a state of readiness to carry on as my only real legacy and potential lasting memory after I am gone. My last photo taken. My last sketch complete. My final word penned and saved. No letters left to write. No goodbyes left to speak. No one left to hug. To be ready now, and at a moment's notice, to loosen my grip when life is done all at once, and then fall into darkness without a single backward glance or backward thought, or longing backwards memory. Likewise, to be prepared if I am no longer able to care for myself due to infirmity or old age.

2. **MAKE GOOD AND EFFECTIVE USE OF TIME AND RESOURCES**

To make good use of these few moments right now, and to dwell very little on past utilization, other than to use such memory to inform my judgment in the direction of improved forward progress. To also make good use of whatever resources are at my disposal, not just for increase, but to spend, share, give, or apply these resources well, and in ways which are in accord with my life objectives and principles. An especially good use of time are self-sustaining interests—namely, occupations of mind and time which are ends in themselves. Listening to the sound of rain is an example. As is reading a good poem. Walking the dog is another. So too, tucking myself into bed. Activities which are more difficult to remember tomorrow, yet which are very easy to live today.

Below are examples of some of the things I would like to be caught doing when death comes at last to utterly snuff out my light:

- Breathing slow and measured breathes
- Controlling my emotions
- Thinking and acting deliberately
- Remembering and acting upon my responsibilities
- Eating well and very little
- Helping others
- Being attentive to my family
- Providing good value to my employer
- Learning something startlingly new
- Reading an excellent book
- Memorizing poetry which moves me
- Listening to a good lecture, discussion, or debate
- Challenging what I believe

248

- Changing my mind for good reason
- Admitting that I was wrong
- Apologizing when necessary
- Becoming uncomfortable
- Withstanding discomfort
- Suffering well and longer than I thought I could
- Standing, walking, swimming or simply moving
- Making a pet happy
- Picking up litter
- Accurately recounting the idea of another
- Sleeping deeply
- Discovering I am wrong
- Remembering death
- And the best use of time of all (also possibly the hardest)—just being present and aware...

3. DEVELOP AND MAINTAIN GOOD AND SOUND LIFE PRINCIPLES

"Do justice, and let the skies fall."

-Roman proverb

I will secure early in life, good rules to live by, objectives and principles which are accurate and true. I will then dedicate some time each day to using, testing, and refining these objectives and principles. Over time, I will make a small catalog of only the soundest truths I have found, which I will then number and recount each day for the purpose of further discover and self-guidance. Finally, I will share what I have found through the example of my words and actions, and my best effort of living a good and sound life.

4. **CULTIVATE GOOD EMOTIONAL REACTIONS**

I will take control of my emotions such that these inform my living more than control it. Feelings and reactions will then become life councilors, rather than rulers and chiefs. Through this effort I will create and reflect a life of equanimity through inward control and a resulting outward peace. I will remember that life is lived as one upon a seashore, noting and living according to the tides; which fall now with feelings of low regard towards our purpose, and meaning, and well-being; followed later by rising spirits and outlook, with the fresh, clean flood flowing in—temporary, here for a very short season, before the ebb comes again to frustrate, confuse, and concern us in an always recurring cycle of lows and highs, and lows again once more.

5. **PERFORM GOOD ACTIONS**

My deeds should be worthy of a life spent working to pass each day as an improvement, not only for myself and my family, but also for those with whom we share life now, as well as those in the future who will receive this common inheritance.

6. **RECOGNIZE TRUE LIMITS AND TRUE OPPORTUNITY**

I will strive to live life in honest recognition of my true scope of control, which extends no further than my thoughts, actions and reactions, and the consequences these might entail. I will ask myself how I may craft favorable ends from any circumstance. What misfortune do I not have the power to fashion into some instrument of virtue? Is it death now at the door? Do not bar the way. For the hour of our meeting is truly at hand, and I will not attempt to detain in vain, any will, force or consequence which is truly beyond my control. And what role apathy in my discernment and feign engagement with a universe beyond the scope of my small control? And what reach must I attempt beyond the near, pale illumination of reason?

7. ONE THING SLOWLY

Do only one thing at a time and do that thing slowly. I will try hard to never take on two activities or entertain two thoughts at the same time. In addition, I will pursue each activity or thought slowly. If I find this limit difficult to maintain, then clearly, I have accepted more responsibility than I can reasonably handle. Of course, there will be times I am unable to maintain this workload or ratio due to deadlines or other necessities. However, in hindsight I will try to identify where I went wrong, and how I managed to let my workload or responsibilities get so out of control that I had to multitask. I will do this in order to try and avoid making the same mistake in the future. I will then learn from my error and become more mature for the effort. The benefit of this objective may be self-evident in my improved ability to focus my attention on whatever is most important in the current moment. Moving and thinking slowly further improve these efforts by ensuring I make good and well-considered choices and actions which are less prone to mistake or costly redo. Over time, I will become able to do more with less and make better ends of whatever means I find and enjoy a more relaxed and considered living at both work and play.

8. BALANCE

"To have the management of one's own mind is a great art, that might be attained in a considerable degree by experience and habitual exercise."

-Dr. Johnson

The difficult thing of keeping upright and straight, and walking forward without too much stagger or sway. It's no easy thing when ambush comes our way, or when our limbic system kicks in with suggestions, drives and sudden emotions we did not expect. Like a tightrope walker stepping carefully on the narrow way, with open expanse below and sway and movement everywhere about. I will strive to not fall just now or tomorrow. And I will walk and think each day ready for whatever winds or blinding sunlight or rain or sudden storm or long expanse of burning sun or the tedium of no change may come my way.

Thirty-five principles

1. **PRINCIPLE OF WAR**
   I rise each morning taking arms first against my own philosophy and beliefs and secondly against the philosophy and beliefs of others. I will suffer no unsound or unjust objective or principle to survive my honest, reasoned critique, no matter the consequence to my sense of peace, comfort, or abiding world view. I will equally yield to the warfare of another against my precious truths when these are shown to be unsound or dishonest in any way.

2. **PRINCIPLE OF REASON**
   Sub-principles: honesty, objectivity, doubt & humiliation

   "The life of reason is best and pleasantest, since reason more than anything else is man. So too this life is also the happiest."

   -Aristotle

Reason is my first instrument of reconciling hypothesis with truth. To be effective, I must be honest with myself and others regarding what I know and do not know; and make pains to view the world objectively, without coloring reality too much with imagination fortified of want, or need, or fear, or the normalizing pressure of authority, tradition, and unfounded consensus. Doubt is my default stance and starting point for every new venture of inquiry. And humiliation at my own realized folly the surest sense that I am on the right track of correcting my own wrongs. Reason at its best is a tool of self-immolation, turned first inward as I seek to burn away the chaff and waste of unprincipled living, and then outward in resistance of our species' less worthy answers to the mysteries of life.

3. **THE HOMUNCULUS**
This is the small, mute, and hidden man within my head. The imaginary mortal who seemingly pulls my levers and strings, and hints at my opinions and judgments, and who must die utterly upon the failure and dissolution of my person. The homunculus is as imaginary as a soul, though a much better vehicle to remind myself that consciousness is nothing more than another organ of my body, serving a particular function, and as subject to corruption and death in the end as my spleen, liver, or any other bodily organ.

4. **ANCHORHOLD**
The place where we suffer and die

There is an inward architecture which we create through the fact and consequence of our decisions and actions, which becomes the scaffolding structure of the inner man or woman who others may dimly see when they look us square in the eyes; perceiving a light or darkness within which shines or empties in proportion to the effort we have made to not just live, but to live well, and in accord with our perceived nature and better inclination. We fail utterly when we build our inner world solely guided by the prescribed blueprint precedent of others, which guidance may suffice to create grand and stately outward living, but may leave us inwardly hollow and empty in the end, when we are alone within our outer world, and we look at what we have, and do possess, and have made; and we wonder what we may have seemingly missed—and if somehow there may be more? Why are we so outwardly filled yet so inwardly empty? Our home then, a stable and impressive castle of outward success and seemingly worthwhile achievement and acclaim, resting upon an inner foundation of shifting sand.

5. THE HOME OF GOOD AND EVIL

"Activity in accordance with virtue is virtue."

-Aristotle

A catalog of right and wrong maintained by that little mortal within my head, containing both opinion and judgment, and suggestive of a platform of subjective responsibility. The Homunculus owns this list and has the responsibility to develop and vet its contents; as well as reconcile these with the reasoned opinions of others. Good and evil then become perspective and opinion, dangerously subjective, yet also subject to the truth-finding powers of reason, honesty, and objectivity. Argument and discussion are the tools of reconciliation when such opinions differ, and consensus reached in this way has more authority and force than the proclamations and commandments of a thousand fictitious gods.

6. THE PRINCIPLE OF PURPOSE
Sub-principles: Biology, duty, virtue & mission

"Active in indolence, abroad who roam
In quest of HAPPINESS which dwells at HOME,
With vain pursuits fatigued, at length will find
Its real dwelling is a virtuous mind."

-Dr. Zimmerman

My first purpose is to live and reproduce, before then dying and getting the hell out of the way. I will also perform my duty: thirty years of life dedicated to improved societal ends, as well as twenty-five years of service to my kid, which work is largely complete when she is done with school. Beyond that, it is up to each of us to decide what our own personal purpose will be. For myself, I select the pursuit of virtue—where virtue is defined as a life lived in furtherance of the well-being of thinking things. And my mission is the series of goals I set for myself to achieve over the successive years of my life.

7. THE ATOMIC PRINCIPLE
Sub-principles: dissolution and emergence

"All things change to fire,
and fire exhausted
falls back into things."

-Heraclitus

Everything in the universe is bits and pieces...flowing and changing...forever transforming and becoming. So too you and me—here for a bit, soon to pass, soon to dissolve, never again this thing once more. When remembering this

255

principle, I will often pick up a handful of sand or dirt to let sift through my fingers in the blowing wind.

8. THE PRINCIPLE OF NATURE

"A beast's track through the brush..."

Everything and everyone has some qualities and character which define what they are, and what they are about. This nature, combined with perspective and will, is their paradigm and operational guide. The demands of Biology are a mandate deep and sound from the perspective of survival, and the continuance of our kind. I ask myself at every chance what is the nature of the things I will meet and interact with today? What are the natures of the people I know and with whom I share life? And what is my own nature? What am I made of and where am I going? Knowing these things will help me to engage better and more reasonably with everyone and everything.

9. THE PIRATE RIDE

"And he's awake who thinks himself asleep."

-John Keats

There is no good reason to imagine we are anything but atoms and molecules, and compounds and organs, and muscles and limbs, and brain and mind—instantiated through energy borrowed of the sun and the internal heat of the earth in alignment with the inertia of the universe. That is it. In a sense—a very crude sense—we are complex chemical reactions: natural processes unwinding through brief years, months, and days towards some conclusion which a sufficiently powerful computer algorithm might one day plot and predict. We are decision engines, driven by the universe at large. In a sense, our destiny was always set, with our deliberations and decisions being just some distinct moments of seeming agency along our chemical unwinding from conception to death—a pathway we could hardly avoid or choose otherwise; a route decided not by us, but instead by the complex orchestrations of a universe which delivered us into life, and mindlessly conspires during every moment we live to nudge and jostle us into every decision and action we vainly think our own. Life a purposeless river-like meander. We live, we experience, we think, we decide, and we move—but never truly of our own volition, and always on the path of our law-bound chemical unwinding. Life, therefore, is like a Disney theme park pirate ride: an unintentional horror, joy, and amusement in which the robot pirates and the living riders are one. We live our lives then along seemingly invisible tracks we can never jump or escape, for we lack utterly the will to do anything but stay our course. And though we can make any decisions we like; we can never have made any decisions other than the ones we did.

10. **THE PRINCIPLE OF MATURITY**
Sub-principles: wisdom, fortitude & integrity

Maturity is a finely curated collection of experience gained of life trials both succeeding and failing and recalled with some accuracy and honest consideration toward improved future ends. Wisdom is the soil where such considerations are ploughed, while fortitude is the will and persistence to see the harvest through, and integrity maintains our sound constitution.

11. THE SOCIAL PRINCIPLE
Sub-principles: diplomacy, justice & conspiracy

"Society is the true sphere of human virtue."

-Dr. Johnson

Human beings generally operate in pursuit of our own well-being and the well-being of one another. We can survive alone—though we rarely flourish in solitude, and we risk that whatever understanding and wisdom we gain in deep and persistent disconnect may not be easily communicated or translated to others; and may become irrelevant babble despite perhaps being true. Therefore, find one another, and make good effort to be together and share ideas. Go alone at times...but always return to be with others. I will become a diplomat and ambassador to not only the familiar, but also the strange and new. I will strive always with others towards sane and just ends. Become a man or woman of one another. We will conspire together towards what we perceive and decide is good. These are lofty goals; something I struggle daily to attain.

12. THE PRINCIPLE OF FAMILY
Sub-principle: catalyst

Our people make up the context of our lives in terms of purpose, obligation, mission, feedback, support and ultimately the best and almost intangible part of being alive. We begin with the people to whom we are born, the chance family which we gain by accident of birth. We grow then with the family we later decide, our friends and our partners and our spouse and the children we in turn together make. From these we gain our decided mission

and our direction and our guidance forward; for better or
worse, for richer or poorer, in sickness and in health, 'till
death or very good cause do us part. Without this
connection and circumstance we can still live a rich and
meaningful life, though the way may be harder at times as
we strive with less mandate, catalyst perhaps, to compel us
through thick and thin, less necessity to push us out the
door to our jobs on days when we'd rather not, and
through many years and decades of hard work, sacrifice
and giving—the very selfless endeavors which yield virtue
from the dawning chaos of our life's rising and falling and
one day utterly failing. And if, once dead, we've left behind
the fact and echo of our virtuous living within the "family"
we formed and supported and maintained, then our life
will hardly have been lived in vain, even if everything is
eventually, one day in vain.

13. PUBLIC SPEAKING
*Sub-principles: best words, prudence, felicity, eloquence,
literature, rumor & gossip*

*"To him that ordereth his conversation aright
will I shew the salvation of God."*

-Psalm 50:23

Speak and communicate always as though any person
being spoken of is standing directly before us and attentive
to our every word. In this way we shall not gossip or pass
idle time at the expense of another. Use few words and just
the right words to cautiously convey our meaning in
alignment with our thoughts and emotion, avoiding verbal
flourish unnecessary to our intent, or the adornment of our
ideas with words irrelevant to our more Spartan meaning.
Read great writing for the benefit of example and

precedent. And never spread stories or trade in the misfortune or folly of others.

14. **TEMPERANCE**
   Sub-principles: suffering, simplicity & apathy

   "Keep your tongue and your belly under control."

   -Anthony the Great

   Temperance is the controlled consumption of all things, such as food and drink, work, and play, and even our thoughts and emotions. I will strive to recognize these consumables and then measure out a reasonable portion for myself and then strive to consume very little of that. Such worthy living naturally entails some suffering when we deny ourselves our wants, though a simple life makes this easier when the denial becomes part-and-parcel of our habits and conditioned response. I will then apply apathy towards the intemperance of others, as well as any personal misadventure which is beyond my control. I will recognize my own excess and that of my peers and then use apathetic indifference as a buffer to prevent my consumption of the *Feast of Offal* (principle number 18).

15. **LIFE WILL NOT GO WELL**

   "The course of a stream..."

   I'll be damned if I don't nearly always stumble, trip, slip or otherwise get bounced around, turned backwards, and have the hardest time keeping a straight line towards the objects and ends I set myself to reach or achieve. It's like life is this imperfectly evaluated landscape of changing textures, seasons, and weather; where winds suddenly gust from one side and slippery ice appears on the ground in a shady hollow or a lurking beast stalks and jumps from behind and a friend hails us demanding our time and attention and our bodies complain and yield to fatigue, disease and our ever-increasing weakness of capacity and uncertainty regarding want. That we ever get anywhere we've set out for is an amazing feat, demonstrative of strong object principles, seemingly indefatigable will and a wisdom arrived at by way of experience, reflection, and resolve. Life will not go well. But we certainly can if we try.

16. **THE HORROR SHOW**
The recognized consequence of a universe unfolding beyond reach of our care or ministrations, and the awful evidence that there is no overarching management or oversight beyond the descriptive record we make and share with one another of how things operate, and the necessity which physics, chemistry and time does seemingly demand of us all. At last, we stand with our hands at our sides and our mouths agape and our minds at wits end as the unfolding tale of what is moves on without notice or care of what we want, or think is good, or right, or simply humane. It just moves forward, leaving everyone behind. We will all be left behind in the wake of horror...

17. **THAT WHICH MUST BE BORNE**
Sub-principle: Hand on the tiller

Life presents us with various burdens of many sorts: tasks, duties, responsibilities, as well as circumstances both apprehended and unexpected which we must shoulder, lift and carry despite our will, want, attitude, health, or even our desire. These are the things which we simply must do

261

to fulfill our living mandate. Sure, some choose to not carry such burdens, though they do so not without consequence. Therefore, as long as this is what we must be and do and how we must live, then why not press forward with a smile and eyes lifted towards the sun and the stars and the light which is the better part of our lives. Let us press on despite the weight; move forward in spite of our fatigue; and live on, while mindful and feeling and suffering our weak bodies, frail minds, and inevitable consequent death.

"Steady on course!" declares the master from the deck. "Hold the rudder tight against the wind, and the against current, and your fear, and your doubt, and upset and sense of drift and loss and ambush even by the forces of seeming Nature—and the draw of the seeming Fates towards the maelstrom at port side and the Siren rocks starboard." "Quick!" declare the crew "Lash the master to the mast and unstop his ears before we ourselves shut up our own hearing with wax and throw all our weight to hold the ship straight on course." Thus, we learn the secrets of the song of the demon sea hags while keeping our vision and direction intact against their sway. Will we soon enough go down and drown within the sea? Of course we will...but not before we first sail like men.

18. THE FEAST OF OFFAL
The banquet of our suffering

"A fool uttereth all his mind: but a wise man keepeth it in till afterwards."

-Proverbs 29:11

This strange meal consists of the waste and by-product of unreasoned and unprincipled living, which we sometimes discard like filth where we live, think and act. Every time we become confused, frustrated, upset, or angry, and we take pains to let all the world know, we are then spilling out our personal offal onto the world, spreading the filth of our hot, raw emotions onto everyone within range of our upset. The curious thing is that so many then take up the filth we've flung at them, to then consume it with seeming relish, making themselves immediately sick in the process, and causing them to begin their own reciprocal Feast of Offal. And thus, it spreads, from one to another, throughout the waking day, and even at night while we dream our emotions into life; an awful banquet of filth, soiling deeply our peace and better living, poisoning our lives and the lives of everyone we know. I wish to cover my mouth and nose instead. To filter out the foul excess of undisciplined thought and living. To temper my emotions and my careless consumption of the emotions of others. I will neither offer, nor consume, the feast.

19. THE PRINCIPLE OF DISTRACTION
Sub-principle: Playing in the sand

> *"What is the course of the life*
> *of mortal men on the earth?—*
> *Most men eddy about*
> *Here and there—eat and drink,*
> *Chatter and love and hate,*
> *Gather and squander, are raised*
> *Aloft, are hurl'd in the dust,*
> *Striving blindly, achieving*
> *Nothing, and then they die—*
> *Perish; and no one asks*

Who or what they have been
More than he asks what waves
In the moonlit solitudes mild
Of the midmost Ocean, have swell'd,
Foam'd for a moment, and gone."

-Matthew Arnold

At every turn in life we desire not to see. We turn our heads to look, not away, but towards, something which might cause us not to see. The thing we do not want is to observe the emptiness which resides behind and before and between and within it all. We do not wish to sense the negative silence of the universe's apparent vacuum of purpose. We do not want to know that death is forever beyond a nighttime soon to come which we can neither know nor avoid. And so, we busy ourselves with school and work and family and friends and hobbies and interests and gossip and joy and sorrow and peace and gratitude and anxiety and angst and ecstasy and the very fact of the observance that we are alive. Anything... Anything at all will do... Anything to avoid the awful aspect and great indifference of a soulless universe without god.

Yet more and more, I am less inclined to fill the empty with my own fearful, distracted voice. Increasingly preferring substance to filler, though substance is harder to find and still harder to hold, leaving me often with nothing at all. But I am alright with that now. I'm at last better without the distraction of life and death which I know is not.

Nevertheless, I continue to play in the sand, looking for sand, digging for sand, everywhere sand—like all of us, distracted by sand in our quest for sand; so much busyness, so much fuss and bluster, so much restless apparent life.

20. AGENCY AND THE GREAT INDIFFERENCE

"I looked at the stars, and considered how awful it would be for a man to turn his face up to them as he froze to death, and see no help or pity in all the glittering multitude."

-Charles Dickens

Every individual life is an agent, and the products of its living are its artifacts. Subtract these away and what's left is the vast landscape of *The Great Indifference*— characterized by an incapacity to observe or maintain any thought or opinion towards well-being, an utter lack of regard towards joy or suffering, a god-less backdrop of unthinking, inanimate substance and time.

21. THE BEST SEAT IN THE HOUSE

"I have learnt, in whatever state I am,
therewith to be content."

-St. Paul

This place and time where I am now will suffice. I will have peace where, and who I am, at this time, and doing whatever engages my necessity and motive and the pursuit of virtue. Meanwhile, I will also strive towards better ends for myself and others, not as a replacement of my current circumstances and work, but rather as a natural improvement upon these.

22. THE RESTLESS MAN
Sub-principle: Diminished Potency

"Travelling is a fool's paradise. We owe to our first journeys the discovery that place is nothing. At home I dream that at Naples, at Rome, I can be intoxicated with beauty and lose my sadness. I pack my trunk, embrace my friends, embark on the sea, and at last wake up in Naples, and there beside me is the stern Fact, the sad self, unrelenting, identical, that I fled from. I seek the Vatican, and the palaces. I affect to be intoxicated with sights and suggestions, but I am not intoxicated. My giant goes with me wherever I go.

-Ralph Waldo Emerson

There must be someplace better than here... Somewhere I can go to find satisfaction... If only I hadn't made those earlier bad choices in life: hadn't gone left when I should better have gone right, or straight, or heck even back—if I'd only decided to spend my life with that other person, or stayed in that other city, or taken a different job... Any direction at all besides the direction I went, which led me now to this settled, safe, dull, and unsatisfying place and life. Oh, how I want now that something else. Maybe I can convince those I'm bound to here, the people who expect and deserve my life with them here, the ones I've committed to, that there is someplace better than here for us all? Maybe I can drag them all along with me, the spouse, the kids, the dog and cat. We'll throw away all this crap we've gained cluttering the garage, things we bought attempting to settle our restless ticking, things which quell nothing for more than a day or a week, gaining us only further loss in their successful gain. Oh, damn it all to hell! Why I am I stuck here in this place and doing this job and

266

living in this home and behaving this way when none of it is really, truly me?? Why did I agree to this arrangement? Why can't I get away?

This is what we think. And this is what we do. When nature prompts us to new horizons. Nature has wired the young to press boundaries, to go beyond limits, and to cross over mountains to find new places where more and better might be found. This instinct and drive are one of the ways we survive. It's how humans spread across the globe. It's why, while we went extinct in one place, others of us lived on elsewhere. Not everyone is built this way, men more than women I suspect, but both sexes to be sure. And there will be no peace to those who are so driven. The only peace being the arrival of old age. Expect some relief in the mid-fifties or thereabouts, about the time—and in relative proportion to—your waning bodily potencies. Until then, suffer if you ignore the call to the Path. And even then, suffer on.

23. THE PATH OF WILDNESS
Sub-principles: Shadow Dividend & Ulysses' Ride

"The direction of our first inclination..."

At every life crossroads I will assess the fact that a decision must be made, and then determine how much time I have to make it, and then collect my facts and consider the options, and then decide at the appointed time. If my facts are insufficient, and there really is no more time, then I will listen to my gut instinct, let it have its say, and then perhaps move in that direction, confident in having made the best evaluation I could, in a reasonable amount of time, and with the resources and facts at my disposal. I will be alright with whatever outcome—even if the next end is death. And

267

I will beware the hard benefits which come of such change, the improvements which hurt, but which can be had in no other way; the Shadow Dividends of the pain of change and the loss of what is no longer needed. And I will suffer well through the decided pathway, like Ulysses riding the storm and temptation which he chose for his own.

24. THE GREAT LIFE ADVENTURE

"Leaves blown in the wind..."

"He who continues the same course of life in the same place, will have little to tell."

-Dr. Johnson

Embark when you are young upon that beckoning dream and adventure. Let it be the centerpiece and point of reference for the man or woman who you will become. Let the experience inform and guide your active philosophy as well as the development of your own living objectives, principles, and standards.

25. THE RISK OF AVOIDING RISK
Sub-principles: risk management, becoming the person you are, and to err on the side of family

Life presents us with a variety of risks which we must attend to. Our parents and society commonly advise us to get an education, find a good job, and then settle down to a safe and sane life making and raising babies with a decided, worthy another. These are good, responsible things to do. But I offer there is a deeper risk which also needs attention; the risk of living a long and healthy life without allowing ourselves the chance to develop and engage our deeper self, or experiencing life without much challenging adventure, or living in such a way as to keep too much distance from the risks which yield the rich and satisfying reward of discovery, maturity, survival, and growth. So, attend to both types of risk: the practical aims of school, work, family, security, and money, as well as perhaps the less practical, though often quite worthwhile, risk of not becoming the person or living the life of our dreams. Avoid the trap of managing risk to the extent of walling ourselves completely into our own safe, secure, and familiar coffin, becoming who we have settled for; though when in doubt, always err on the side of family—even if such living might at times feel like a coffin—as such efforts are usually in alignment with our deeper and perhaps our only true life mandate and purpose; namely, getting our genes successfully into the next generation, passing, as Emerson might say, our ripened being into tomorrow.

26. SIN AND DAMNATION

Sub-principles: falsity, credulity, faith, superstition, dogma, authority, rumor and gossip

It is a sin to invest our expectations with hope, which may be corrupted or foiled by fortune. It is also a sin to believe things without good reason; to acquiesce for the sake of comfort, or security, or peace, or to simply avoid the discomfort of not knowing. The penalty for this sin is damnation, in the here-and-now, which is the only time we will ever really have. Damned for our unreasoned want. Damned for our unreasoned belief. Damned for our thoughtless, careless communications.

27. COMPLETE OBLIVION

Sub-principles: no final reunion, no final reconciliation, and no final justice

"So man lieth down, and riseth not: till the heavens be no more, they shall not awake, nor be raised out of their sleep."

-Job 14:12

Soon the light within the mind will wink out. My life will come to an end. The storehouse of my memory will lose its electricity, which is the means of its maintenance and growth. The columns of my mental library and lyceum will quickly crumble and fall, the roof cave in, the foundations turn to sand. The philosopher is gone, evaporated to atoms. There will be then no last reunion with loved ones, no reconciliation of hard, careless or misspoke words, no satisfaction of wanting justice. The whole thing simply blows away with the new morning's breeze.

28. THE SEASON OF PHILOSOPHY

"Philosophy wields her own authority; she appoints her own time and does not allow it to be appointed for her."

-Seneca the Younger

Think and record your thoughts while you can. See how the sun is fading now, dropping near the horizon? You will not survive the coming night. If you fail to record your words today—right now—they will never come again. Or maybe, if the words arrive again in some new form some distant day hence, will you have the body, will or constitution to record what you hear? Will your mind still function well enough to put the words together in the correct order? Will you have enough energy then for the effort? Will your hands perhaps tremble too much, or your medicine dull your nerves, or your broken self simply refuse to cooperate? Will you remain tuned to the muse? These are very real risks. So instead, keep a pad and pencil handy now, or a recorder, or camera, and pull yourself aside when the muse speaks, attend to her words, and prepare your thoughts and philosophy as best you can, while you can.

29. SCRIPTWRITING

Life presents us always until death with an almost clean and clear canvas of whatever available time we've left. We may use this canvas to either live whatever life happens to us, or to take more active control of our days, hours, and minutes in order to seemingly manage and guide our path according to our seeming will, and in alignment with our hard won and decided values, goals, and best practice. This "scriptwriting" requires effort and imagination, as well as optimism if we are to aim our living in the perceived and decided direction of virtue, and to make the most of whatever brief days we have yet the chance to live, experience and hopefully enjoy.

30. BULLSEYE AIM

Our best ambition is to achieve our goals and objectives to the extent that we can feel our effort is complete. That is often a pretty high mark, even with a pessimist's aim. The fact is we frequently fall short, well short, or at least short enough to cause us to bluster or regret that we even tried.

For myself, I will be satisfied if I have made a good and honest effort. There is really otherwise no time to lose.

31. THE UPHILL CLIMB
Sub-principle: The Open Ocean Swim

I will rise each morning and turn my attention to the uphill grade. To the slope which leads up. To the path which resists my climb yet yields ever widening horizons with each step forward. I will move forward and up. I will rarely stop, and I will never willingly go back or even cast a longing backwards glance at the places I've been and have left behind.

Another way to look at this is from the perspective of my life by the sea, where sometimes, I slip alone into the ocean to swim far out to deep water and then along the shore. The water is deep out there. And the waves incessant; pushing me now up and then back and over and across as I make my best line along the distant shore. No matter how the sea might rock or jostle my body, I carry on. I keep swimming. And when a larger wave foils my attempt to take in a breath of air, filling my mouth instead with salt seawater, I only sputter and spit and yet carry on. I swim through the sea with a steady resolve, apathetic to the sea, while nonetheless engaged upon and within it. This is the uphill and steady climb forward. This is the Open Ocean Swim.

32. ARENA AND UTILITY
Every place and situation are an opportunity to practice and refine our objectives and principles. Ask yourself at every point through the day what utility and good end might be found for the employment of your reason and

272

philosophy, which must be forever alert, skeptical, and active. Life is the arena. Our objectives and principles are our utilities.

33. nothing IS enough
Not relying on things for our well-being

"Frugality is not only the basis of
quiet, but of beneficence."

-Dr. Johnson

We start out life in pursuit of whatever might satisfy our aching desire to become sated at the banquet of life. Education, career, friendship, family, and belief are each in turn stuffed into the yawning crevasse opening onto an indifferent universe hard at work exchanging order for night, a cosmos incapable of sympathy to our plight, without pity for our pain, with no awareness or interest regarding our dreams. We try and we try, doing everything we think we should, to no avail and no relief, nothing ever enough, nothing ever being quite enough; until one day...we realize that we are saved when we discover that—*nothing IS enough.*

34. THE PRINCIPLE OF FUN
Sub-principles: hope & retrospect

"Then I commended mirth, because a man
hath no better thing under the sun..."

-Ecclesiastes 8:15

Along the way we might become overly focused on the pursuit of living well such that we neglect to enjoy the fact that we are alive. Be gay, be jolly, have fun! Find friendship, and community, and family and things to do which might make us smile and laugh and sleep well and hard and with a smile on your face. Live such a life that the mortician must ask your heirs if they wish him to wipe the death mask grin from your face before the funeral service begins. Bring to your death a good and happy life as a warm, fading spark of light and life glowing down into the seemingly infinite sea of darkness and gloom.

35. **BEING READY**

Be prepared at all times for anything and nothing. Regarding anything, be especially ready for big things with enduring consequences like education, marriage, children and old age. Go as far as you can with your education; that you study is more important than what you study. Pick someone who shares your core values; looks, hobbies, and all the rest are secondary. Each of your children gets at least twenty-three years of your life; be ready for that. Regarding nothing, be ready for peace; it's harder than it seems.

Today's thought and action plan

The last part of my daily Good Life Meditation is some reflection on the coming day, and how I might make best use of the time, and what issues I may face. I also give some thought to the people I will interact with, and their natures, and the natures of the places and circumstances I will visit and engage. I typically then conclude this activity by admonishing myself to think and act this day in a deliberate and purposeful manner, watching over my thoughts and husbanding my actions, while being regardful of the impact and consequence of my every decision and substantive move. I conclude by asking myself if I am today ready to die? Are my affairs in order? Are my relationships sound? And is my life's work complete? And if the answer to any of these three questions is no, then I add some steps to my day to do what is needed to get these nearer to yes.

This entire process of The Good Life Meditation requires about ten minutes if I do it in my head, and between 25 and 40 minutes if I do it out-loud. I typically go longest, and do my best job, when I have the camera running and I know I will upload the video. Sharing such videos is never easy, as it is rather embarrassing to talk openly with the world about my ideas, issues, and challenges, though the email feedback I get always makes the process quite worthwhile.

Our story

We all need a story to tell and to make of our lives. We need something to be and something to strive and live for, and people for whom we are there and who are there for us. Dedicate some time each day then, before the sun is fully risen, to reflect on what story our life does tell, and what story might be remembered of us after we are gone, even if such memory is only found in the echo and reverberating influence of our deliberate and earnest efforts to live the best life we see fit.

Notes from my muse

Section Hashtag Legend
The following hashtags (#) are used to identify Good Life objectives, principles and other concepts covered in this book and as they apply to "blurbs" within this section and used with my blog.

- #Death – To be always ready to die
- #Time – The good and effective use of time
- #Life – Develop and maintain good life principles
- #Reactions – Cultivate good emotional reactions
- #Actions – The performance of good actions
- #Limits – Recognition of true limits and opportunity
- #Apathy – A sub-objective of true limits & opportunity
- #One – Do just one thing and slowly
- #War – The Principle of War
- #Reason – The Principle of Reason
- #Homunculus – The Principle of the Homunculus
- #Anchorhold – The Principle of the Anchorhold
- #Good – The Home of Good and Evil
- #Purpose – The Principle of Purpose
- #Virtue – A sub-principle of Purpose
- #Biology – A sub-principle of Purpose
- #Mission – A sub-principle of Purpose
- #Atomic – The Atomic Principle
- #Nature – The Principle of Nature
- #Pirate – The Principle of The Pirate Ride
- #Maturity – The Principle of Maturity
- #Wisdom – A sub-principle of Maturity
- #Fortitude – A sub-principle of Maturity
- #Integrity – A sub-principle of Maturity

- #Social – The Social Principle
- #Family – The Principle of Family
- #Catalyst – The sub-principle of Catalyst
- #Diplomacy – A sub-principle of Social
- #Justice – A sub-principle of Social
- #Conspiracy – A sub-principle of Social
- #Speaking – Principle of Public Speaking
- #Temperance – The Principle of Temperance
- #Suffering – A sub-principle of Temperance
- #Simplicity – A sub-principle of Temperance
- #NotWell – Principle of Life Will Not Go Well
- #Horror – The Principle of the Horror Show
- #Borne – The Principle That Which Must be Borne
- #Offal – The Feast of Offal
- #Distraction – The Principle of Distraction
- #Indifference – Agency and The Great Indifference
- #Seat – The Best Seat in the House
- #Restless – The principle of The Restless Man
- #Path #Wildness – The Path of Wildness
- #Dividend – A sub-principle of The Path of Wildness
- #Ulysses – A sub-principle of The Path of Wildness
- #Adventure – The Great Life Adventure principle
- #Risk – The Risk of Avoiding Risk
- #Sin – The principle of Sin and Damnation
- #Faith – A sub-principle of Sin
- #Oblivion – The principle of Complete Oblivion
- #Philosophy – The Season of Philosophy principle
- #Scriptwriting – The Principle of Scriptwriting
- #Bullseye – The principle of Bullseye Aim
- #Uphill – The principle of The Uphill Climb
- #Swim – A sub-principle of The Uphill Climb
- #Arena – The principle of Arena and Utility

- #Nothing – Principle of nothing IS enough
- #Fun – The Principle of Fun
- #Stoic – Stoic ideas

Our most lasting value is reflected less in deadlines met, or goals achieved, than virtuous commitments fulfilled. Define what constitutes the aim of virtue, and let this pursuit and fulfillment be your highest end.

#Time #Purpose #Virtue

~

Beware any feigned virtue which cloaks its mandate in tradition, faith, or dogma. Any truth with something to hide, or which cannot stand alone without insubstantial aids, deserves to let fall under the weight of its own weak folly.

#War #Reason #Virtue #Sin #Faith

~

Apathy becomes a virtue the moment it is applied to events and circumstance beyond our control. I'm apathetic to the desert heat, though I take pains to protect myself from its effect. I apply apathy in good measure to the morning traffic, while reminding myself to leave for work a little earlier tomorrow. And the cancer which may one day destroy my body, and take my life, is equally deserving no more attendance than the reasonable application of the physician's art, and the competent aid of good council in setting my affairs in order. Instead of worry, my time might be better spent with loved ones and engaged in earnest living. Apathy is our tool and respite from whatever affects us—yet is beyond our control. More powerful than fortitude. More tactful than desire. And far, far more graceful than giving up.

#Death #Time #Limits #Reason #Oblivion #Temperance
#Fortitude #Apathy

~

*But how can I maintain my apathy in the face of the suffering
of others? Do not mistake apathy for indifference, where the
missing quality is caring, or the ability to care. Indifference
simply fails to care; while apathy considers what truly can be
done by us, and then applies its energies towards these more
effective ends. Compassion and apathy coexist well together.
For whom can be a more effective caregiver than the man or
woman who recognizes, guides, and controls their own
emotions and whimsy, and then offers always the most genuine
and heartfelt love?*

#Time #Social #Temperance #Apathy #Indifference

~

*I wrote the lines below to my daughter this morning, who
begins her first day of work at her very first job.*

*We shoulder daily the great apparatus of human endeavor. It
matters little where our hands or minds find purchase, as long
as the grip is firm and engaged towards virtuous ends.*

#Time #Purpose #Virtue #Social #Arena

~

*Very often I only remember to apply apathy after the
opportunity has passed. Today something happened, and*

279

apathy arrived in time to prevent the moment from taking control. I was riding my motorcycle to work in the commuter lane. Traffic in the normal lanes suddenly began to slow, with red brake lights coming on up ahead, and I went on the alert for drivers suddenly veering into my open lane to avoid the growing congestion. This happens often, as drivers frequently ignore the double yellow lines which divide the commuter lane from the normal lanes of traffic, and then fail to see the motorcycle occupying what they think is an empty lane. Sure enough, a dark sedan swings in behind me. It's a safe distance back—no danger of collision—though my ire rises suddenly when I note the driver is alone...in the carpool lane. It's a minor thing—this lane is reserved for motorcycles and cars with two or more occupants—though my mind immediately begins rehearsing an old internal monologue of perceived injustice. How selfish the driver is... How inconsiderate to those who make an effort to arrange carpools, or who drive fuel efficient vehicles. And what of the state of society? Where's the Justice? Have we lost our ethical footing? It's a long rant. Almost a manifesto. But just as I was getting started. Just as the first flush of indignation began to rise in my cheeks. I suddenly remembered apathy...that lesser known or regarded virtue of self-discipline; apathy, the ability to recognize what is—and what is not—within our control, to then administer our attention, thought and action towards ends we can actually achieve, and away from futile anger and needless upset. I caught myself. I saw that I could do nothing in that moment about the inconsiderate lone driver behind me. I became apathetic to his trespass, and in so doing I recovered control of my emotions, my thoughts, and the apparatus of my ethical framework and actions. Instead of fuming at the man, or worse, engaging him in some way, I asked myself what I could do to improve the social circumstance that perhaps led to and even encouraged his action. I decide to write these words, and to share the experience with my daughter. To remind her of the virtue of allegiance to fair and just laws. And to hopefully instill in her some example of life best practices, and the powerful utility of a virtue called apathy. A virtue which helps us recognize true limits; and apply our energies where they can do the most good.

\#Life \#Limits \#Nature \#Offal \#Social \#Temperance \#Apathy

~

Apathy came to my rescue again today. I'd composed and sent an email to the team, in which I neglected to state an important fact which I should not have overlooked. When this was publicly pointed out to me, I immediately felt shame, regret and frustration rising up to twist my heart into a knot. But then I remembered my apathy, which first calmed my nerves, and then helped me to identify the factors surrounding this upset. I was then able to note what was both within and outside my control; the fact of my error could only be corrected, but never removed. To let this mistake take control of my well-being therefore was both foolish and ineffectual. Better to temper my emotion and apply this energy to a quick response, publicly acknowledging my appreciation to the person who provided the correct information, and then to consider steps I could take to avoid such error again. I calmly composed and sent the email. I then collected my thoughts and reminded myself in the future to carefully review complex matters before weighing in with a response. Apathy directed me away from what I could not control—namely the fact of my error—and towards what I could, which was remediation, and the development of new behaviors to help prevent such mistakes in the future.

\#Life \#Actions \#Control \#Nature \#Offal \#Temperance \#Apathy

~

The fact that our species has lifted its head above the fray of tooth and claw, to look around and wonder, to imagine virtue and conceive its worthy ends, does not deny the fight which must, for now, go on, and to which we are amply built to participate.

#Purpose #Virtue #Nature

~

The Feast of Offal is not only an expression of folly and the consequence of unprincipled and undisciplined living, but also a screen and distraction from the fact of indifference, which everywhere pervades.

#Offal #Nature #Indifference

~

Ever since departing from social media, and turning off all mobile notification, save contact from instant messenger, my phone has become a mute, loyal and worthy companion. It no longer disturbs me with tweets, or posts, or likes, or news, or events. It politely answers only when I ask it questions, which leaves me freer to think, and to act, as I see fit. When the phone does buzz, it's always someone I love. Always someone dear. Never a robot. Never an algorithm designed to adjust my thoughts, or behavior, or spending. I'm not a technophobe. Just a man who treasures the possession of his moments.

#Time #Limits #Nature #Social

~

The homunculus is no less an organ of the body than the liver or the spleen.

#Reason #Homunculus #Nature #Oblivion

~

My homunculus resides in a barrel within my head[10]. Though my outward man works, votes, and pays taxes, the inner self sleeps with his back in a crook, and looks out at the sunrise through a gaping round orifice, begging passerby to not block out the sun. He walks the avenues of my mind with bare feet and a torn shirt, or shirtless if the weather is fine. While I attend meetings, my homunculus meanders alone, or with dogs, in search of an honest man. When I dine, he resists hunger with a crust of bread, and a pot of cheese should he wish a feast. One day I will become that better man, that ragged, lean and honest self; when I at last put aside this vain pursuit of living, and choose instead to simply live.

#Limits #Homunculus #Nature #Temperance #Philosophy

~

My homunculus has a ledger. It's a crude journal of inaccurate impressions, vague suppositions and conclusions drawn of far too little experience or fact. This book has a section for good and evil, and even another for right and wrong. The entries are all drawn in bright crayon, as they require color to gain emphasis, being otherwise of so little merit. My homunculus is quite proud of what he's made. He even shares and compares with others, drawing and offering criticism, which he hardly likes. But what more or better could he use to gauge the world?

283

His life is so short, and so imperfect—though he prefers to not be reminded of this fact—that he holds to what he's got with more certainty than merit. That's his fault, though don't expect him to confess it. Few ever do.

#Homunculus #Good #Oblivion #Philosophy

~

Virtue isn't complicated. It's just the pursuit of the well-being of living things. It's making decisions, and performing actions which make life better, in objective, meaningful ways. Clean drinking water, good education, equality between the races and the sexes; clear communication, good medicine, and prioritized attention to the most needy and suffering among us. Well-being also includes the preservation of healthy habitats for wildlife, clean, open spaces for recreation, and the humane and conscientious treatment of those with whom we share the planet. These things can be decided by all of us through reasoned discussion. There's no need of dogma, revelation, or miracle to pursue such ends. Virtue is what we agree is good. And then the doing of it.

#Reason #Purpose #Virtue #Social #Sin

~

Coming back to the USA brought many changes. A new job, new home, new commute, a different diet, new things to do on the weekends; new worries, new challenges, but very few new friends. In fact, almost none. I can probably count on the number of fingers I need to eat a cookie, the people I've become close to since returning to America. My wife probably needs fewer fingers than that. We talk about it sometimes. We both find it a little odd that neither of us has made much effort to cultivate new friendships, or even maintain old. Our daughter on the other hand, has more new friends than we can keep track of. We're meeting or hearing about new people in her life all the time. Yet Yumiko and I have seemingly returned to our base configuration of having just one another. We make no effort to expand, and have little interest to do so. We like things the way they are.

A good weekend these days includes a few meals out as a family, a movie together, some grocery shopping, and lots of free time to just do whatever we want, alone or together. We like it this way. We feel like we're settling into our 50s in a more personal and intimate way than ever before.

A big contributor to this change was my departure from the JVLOG community, which is a Japan-based network of YouTube content creators who often share much of their personal lives online. I shared a lot...over six thousand videos across ten years and twenty channels! Being on the business-end of a camera became a big part of who I was then. It made me feel like I had many more friends than I actually did.

I now enjoy maybe two or three really good conversations a week with people who are not my family. That's enough. I don't want any more good conversations than that. And I certainly don't want any bad conversations, or conversations for just the sake of passing time.

I suspect Yumiko and I will continue to settle in deeper this way. There seems to be a renaissance brewing between us. A rediscovery of the first decade of our life together. A time when we just had one another and nothing else.

I can easily see us going on this way. Watching our teenage daughter grow and go. Devoting our energies to her well-being, *until she needs us little, and then retiring our focus to our own humble living.*

I see a small, one-bedroom apartment by the beach, and within walking distance to downtown. I see a dog. I see some favorite TV shows together, some restaurants we like, movies on Sunday where we spilt a bucket of popcorn. I see me alone in the wild for a day or two every other week, while Yumiko does her thing. I see grandkids and old age. I see helping one another through the difficult last decade. I see a sad goodbye, followed by some time alone for one of us. I see a good life together. But I see very, very few friends from this point forward.

#Time #Limits #Nature #Social #Adventure

~

The Season of Philosophy is that time between The Great Life Adventure and the period of our mental and bodily decline. Wait too long and the words will never come, or have no way to get out.

#Time #Limits #Nature #Adventure #Philosophy

~

The Great Life Adventure is that experience in life when you step from knowledge into ignorance and return with less, and then continue losing more for the rest of your days.

#Time #Limits #Maturity #Temperance #Simplicity #Adventure

~

The experience of The Great Life Adventure is like having a small hole appear in a bag of gold dust we carry everywhere secured to our waist. The gold is our certitude, and the security of our cherished world view, and our knowledge, and everything we believe. It's best if the hole comes early, is very small, and has time to drain away much of our treasure before we realize what we've lost. The adventure was a success if, once discovered, we then make no effort to mend the hole.

#Time #Adventure #Maturity #Fortitude

~

Anxiety is an ambush predator. It takes advantage of sudden, unexpected circumstance or worry to pounce upon our back, thrust its claw into our chest, and twist hard the beating heart which drives its fury. The experience is tangible, tactile, and deadly real. When it happens to me, I usually find myself wishing some retreat, some way to get away, some relief from whatever external happening I imagine is the cause of my anxious worry.

At age fifty-three things have changed. I've learned there's little I can do to alter external circumstances which are beyond my control, and which are the cause of my worry. Simply wishing I was away from the problem is a fantasy, as long as I want to retain my duty and abide my responsibility. Wishing others would be different is likewise folly. As is the demand for justice where no enforceable law has been broken. After all it's not illegal if someone is lazy, incompetent, or simply does not care to do their job well. These things are all largely outside our control. And it's worthwhile to remember this when anxiety strikes. If only to remind ourselves of the bounds of our power and control.

What we DO control is our reaction and response to whatever is happening in the world around us. We decide what we will think, say, or do, in almost every circumstance. We're especially in control of our inner world, which is the place from which our external actions arise. This internal world is the focal point of our power and control, and the realm we must master should we become invincible to external onslaught. Not immortal. Not impervious to pain. But invincible to whatever we recognize as not ours to control.

A very busy workday is our problem if we fail to manage our time well, and let our responsibilities pile. That's our bad. It's good to feel pain in that circumstance. Let it soak in and prompt us to do better. But if the day is madness because some system or process fails, or someone calls in sick, or our boss lays on too much work, or it's a Monday. Then what are we to do beyond reasonable protest and a request for help? If these attempts fail, then our natural response may be to worry.

But this is where things have changed for me. Instead of anxiety, which is a form of fearful standstill in the face of a threat we cannot seem to overcome, why not try temperance, and apathy, and recognizing the nature of others, and the nature of circumstance, and most importantly the true scope and reach of our own power and influence, our own nature.

We temper our anxiety when we deliberately limit our consumption of anxious thinking. This process involves literally pausing before we ingest a thought, to examine it and lay it aside if it is found to be unwholesome. To only consume the thought if it is good and worthy, and helps us towards worthwhile and virtuous ends.

288

Apathy is our tool to disarm whatever is beyond reach of our direct control. This is done by first recognizing our inability to reach the thing, to then let it go, and then plan some contingency or scheme for a better world in spite of the thing, using the powers we do have.

Finally, nature. I ask myself: is it not the nature of lazy people to be lazy? How foolish of me then to continually expect otherwise. Is it not the nature of systems or processes to sometimes fail? Why so distraught then over system or process failure? What about Mondays? Is it not their habit to come once each week between Sunday and Tuesday? If these are true and accurate descriptions of the nature of these things, then let me get over my foolish expectations otherwise. Let me strive to recognize the nature of all things, and though I may cautiously hope for better, I will expect nothing more than their nature. These are the changes which give me better control of worry and anxiety. The tools are: temperance, apathy, and the recognition of the nature of things, along with my own nature, and my desire for reasonable justice and the pursuit of a more virtuous life.

#Reactions #Limits #Nature #Virtue #Justice #Temperance #Limits #Apathy #Oblivion #Stoic

~

Is there any end which can't be reached by faith? This fact should raise our guard. That every world religion uses the same path to a different truth must tell us something about the path. Can they all be right? Can this method not be used to any end? Is there any claim which cannot be believed by faith?

#War #Reason #Sin #Faith

~

Happiness depends upon no factor more than our willingness to be content.

#Limits #Temperance #Stoic

~

The nothing beyond life should be a terror were it not so easily imagined around, or avoided altogether through the petty pleasures, dramas, and distractions of life. I'll busy myself with living, or imagining a life beyond this living, rather than look past life's end to the apparent nothing that offers nothing.

#Limits #Sin #Oblivion #Stoic

~

The claims "God must have done it" or "God must be behind such design or action" have only the power of hypothesis. These statements alone lack sufficient force to persuade anyone other than those already inclined to believe. To convince further, the authors of such statements must next pass their ideas through the rigors of well-designed test and critical evaluation. Simply saying so is insufficient proof. And appeals to faith only weaken the case to the point of disregard.

#War #Reason #Sin #Faith

~

I'll live where I can't touch bottom. Swim always where dark, cold water touches my toes, and where imagined threats eye me hungrily from way down in the deep. I'll leave the shallow waters now and never return. Never again to stand with my chest and arms in the air. Self-condemned to tread water with difficulty until I'm dead, and then to sink at last to the same blind depths where we all must one day go. Never again safe. Never again certain. Always in doubt. Always at peace. Confident only that I've found a good way to live.

#Limits #Oblivion #Adventure

~

Faith is the sin of belief as a means to an end we could not otherwise achieve.

#Sin #Faith

~

It's increasingly evident where I'm now headed. As it's the same place I was going thirty years ago. Only then I'd never have arrived. Not a chance. I had to go the long way 'round.

It's clear to me now there's no direct path from where I was at age 23 to where I am now at 53. I was facing an impossible climb then. It's a lucky thing I changed course at the very last moment. Truly, not a second to lose.

Now I'm clear the rough stuff. It's relatively smooth passage the rest of the way. Even if I live to one hundred. Even if I die soon from accident or disease. Even if I suffer 'till the end of my days. Even if I must watch my loved ones die first.

I'd like to apologize for so much introspection. Yet what else of real value do I have at this, the autumn of my life? I can talk of love, charity and benevolence to others. All good things of course, and things within my power. Yet these are given traits and qualities of any man or woman who has tried to live well and good. That's the reason I write of these other things. Characteristics of a more alien and foreign nature. Things discovered on the path I'd never planned to take, and never knew existed. Never even knew I was on.

#Time #Limits #Virtue

~

I'm watching my mind squirm and wriggle now. It's wants to escape. But it can't go anywhere without me. And I won't let it. I won't agree to what it wants. The experience is a little like a resolute parent watching with folded arms while their child tantrums on the floor.

The part of me that protests is very ancient. Very primitive. And very, very wise. It's not me really, but instead simply the part of my brain developed of millions of years of survival. It's the part of me that's survived every single life and generation from my parents right back to the protozoa which were our common ancestor. This part of me knows danger. Knows how to spot it. Knows what to do to stay safe. And screams at me now to run away.

The warning voice is telling me not to go out to the desert tonight. It remembers the awful experience two weeks back. It knows the heat, and dehydration, and solitude which are waiting to wring my age-weakened body like a sponge.

*I won't listen... And though I respect and appreciate that
warning voice, and the vast epochs of time which give its shrill
words credence. I think I know better now what's good for me.
I know there are far worse things than mere suffering or death.
The Risk of Avoiding Risk.*

#Reason #Nature #Risk #Temperance #Oblivion

~

*Fortune once held sway over my well-being, as I judged myself
blessed or cursed by its caprice. This same force now flails at
me like a child; weak arms pounding little fists at my every
vulnerability, connecting with dull force and vain impact. The
difference is my abandon of well-being as a function of well-
being. Instead now, virtue alone defines and measures my
success or failure in all things. Of this, fortune has no say.*

#Limits #Reason #Purpose #Virtue #Nature #Maturity #Stoic

~

*The withering edifice of my person shall carry all that I am to
the bottom of the sea. There are no lifeboats on this vessel. No
preservers to strap on before the stern goes down. With a little
courage, the band plays on to the last moment. Dark waters
below. One last breath.*

#Time #Death #Reason #Nature #Temperance #Oblivion

~

*There's time aplenty for a well-lived life. With no heaven
above, and no hell below, we are relieved of the dream of*

forever, and free to invest well these few remaining moments.
How well lived the life of a mortal, who reminds themselves
daily, even hourly, that there is no tomorrow.

#Limits #Reason #Virtue #Oblivion #Stoic

~

My years living before the sea. And my years before the rugged
and wild mountains of Japan. Were but like whispered hints
and rumor of my life now before the desert.

#Nature #Adventure

~

The concepts of heaven and an afterlife are more than a
promise of immortality. They serve also as a cache of relief
from our failed mortal dreams, our mistakes, as well as a
promised balm against all current confusion. If only we simply
believe, then our worthy burden shall be relieved, if not now,
then after we've no chance to know otherwise.

#Death #Limits #Sin #Dogma #Oblivion

~

Do you remember the time before your birth? Neither do I.
Then why leave anything on the table with regard to a well-lived
life, when there's no good reason to think we'll find anything
after this life other than the same dark and quiet empty we
didn't know before. Live well. Live honestly. Love...and be
kind to those who share our path. Leave a good and honest
reckoning of our time and trials here before passing at last to

294

eternal dissolution and nothingness. Live the best life possible during the only life we'll seemingly ever know.

#Time #Death #Reason #Social #Oblivion

~

Dogma enjoys no respite from certitude. This fact is only an issue when we realize the gods gain their morals from us.

#Reason #Sin

~

The threat of complacent living. The risk of the settled life. We may die never knowing what really killed us before we were even dead.

#Limits #Risk #Oblivion

~

I'm right on the edge of the desert now. The killer is nowhere in sight. Is it gone now for the night? I feel a strange reassurance now. Strange only because I feel reassured here, in this otherwise threatening place. It's the same comfort we feel when we're safe at home with our loved ones. A deception of sorts. One we never quite outgrow in civilized climes. But out here this feeling is a stranger; an imposter even. The killer will stalk the night tonight here in the desert. Just as it's doing now where you are. Only out here I have a better chance of seeing it come.

#Limits #Risk #Oblivion #Adventure

~

The view from the position of mortality is immediate and clear. There's no fuzzy line to a wished for forever, and no escaping our troubles but to either solve them or wait for them to outlive us. Even humble things become blessings then. Not because they are gifts. But simply because they are.

#Time #Limits #Reason #Oblivion

~

I'll measure my days like a castaway his scarce rations. I'll apportion then but just 24 hours each day, and allow myself just that. I'll tolerate no greedy dreams of excess, nor any waste of these perishable and perishing moments.

#Time #Limits #Reason #Temperance

~

Have you ever gone below decks with your life, to examine your hull's weak and ruptured places, and note the cold water pouring in. To mark the growing depth of intake at your feet, and to listen as your vessel twists and groans with the gathering stress and pressure of incremental decent. Or maybe it's better to remain above decks always. To gaze at heaven and the stars, and to dream of life everlasting.

#War #Atomic #Temperance #Oblivion

~

Ghosts rely on us for their insubstantial substance. They float and haunt only where our imaginations allow. They fade when forgotten, and moan again when another generation takes up their cause. We join their ranks after we're gone. But only if remembrance and circumstance provide a means of resurrection.

There are no ghosts where our imaginations no longer venture. Nothing spectral haunts the desert where forgotten tribes once lived. No phantoms linger upon shipwrecks lost at sea. And the heavens and hells of dead religions are empty of every pious soul and sinner who ever believed.

#War #Reason #Nature #Sin

~

Miracles are attributions of wonder we neither understand nor care to discover. We marvel from a distance, and dismiss the cause and effect before our eyes, or the hard work of natural agents, or the simple marvel of chance, in favor of some reason we can never support, yet which makes us feel good while affirming our own comforting world view.

Meanwhile, the water-cycle receives no credit for the life-giving rains, the doctor's art no attribution for our cure, and the near miss of an auto accident no credit to chance or good driving.

It's a less glorious or interesting thing to take nature on face value. And far less reassuring to our selfish self-interest and sense of importance. If only the universe would truly care and love us. If only we were chosen. Then we could get on with less

worry. Then we can have peace without the hard work of
thinking and discovering for ourselves.

#Reason #Nature #Indifference

~

Life is far more interesting than it is dangerous.

#Limits #Reason #Adventure

~

Both my fear and my courage have increased with age. My fear;
as a result of perceived consequences. And my courage; by way
of running out of time.

#Time #Maturity #Limits #Oblivion

~

It does not matter that I complete a book of Hawthorne,
Melville or Steinbeck when death arrives at last; but that I
simply be upon the page of one of their books, or another of
like quality, as my final act of passing time. I have no objection
to death sneaking up upon me while I am so worthily
employed.

#Time #Limits #Reason #Oblivion

I'll leave you now,
With my small theology...

THE HOME OF FAITH

MY GOD IS A LITTLE GOD

Expecting nothing more...

"We have not yet encountered any god
who is more merciful as a man who
flicks a beetle over on its feet."

-Annie Dillard

I have come to realize that the muse I so often speak of, and which is the source and inspiration for so many of my thoughts, must be the same muse which heralds and inspires the words, music, thought, and motivation of the religious. A distinction though, is that I apply and attribute no animating will to this contrived agency beyond the scope, breadth, force, and power of my own weak and faltering intellect and imagination. It is no wonder then that I neither trust my god's wisdom, guidance, or even its mere existence. My god is a little god, which can neither speak, write, argue, or even think without my own willful cooperation.

Notes from my muse

I told my little god of the desert today. He'd never heard of such a place. I admired his honesty in fessing up his ignorance. This may be one of his stronger traits. He seemed afraid to learn of the solitude in the desert, and he asked me if any gods or spirits might be found there. I told him it seemed there are none in the wastes. I didn't bother explaining it's all wastes.

~

Caring for a very small god isn't unlike tending a young child. Both are convinced of their omnipotence and immortality, and each at times rails at the world with an impressive wrath and fury. The difference being, the child possesses an anger they can truly inflict upon the world, while my little god relies on my belief to achieve even the slightest destructive end.

~

My little god begged me today to believe in him. I think he's become suspicious his immortality is dependent upon my belief and patronage. Did someone tell him of his contingent existence? Has he learned the root cause of his being? How very afraid he must be.

~

I told my little god that we're going to the desert tomorrow. He seemed unsure after I explained the place, carefully, so as to not offend his growing sense of omniscience. I told him the desert was a place for losing what we cherish, and for gaining what we fear. He nodded slowly, muttering something about the need of a temple. I suspect he'll soon be very disappointed.

~

My little god has no sense of his ignorance, which I reckon the greater measure of omniscience.

~

I told my little god about the helpful muse we might meet in the desert tonight and tomorrow. He wasn't at all pleased, and complained of my holding another before him. It didn't help that I explained my muse is dead, and not even real. Such threats he leveled at me then! Maybe when he meets the nothing himself he'll realize how little there is to fear.

~

I've reached the near edge of the deep desert and oh my, it's cold! I didn't come prepared for this, and I've still 100 miles to go before I reach Siberia, and the safety of my desert camp. The sun's just now gone away, and I know the deeper cold is coming. This is scary, just like the summer heat which has now passed was scary. Only this scary burns in a way that brings on shivers and chattering teeth rather than delirium and fatigue. I'll bundle up now as best I can, and turn on the motorcycle's heated handgrips which are a peripheral comfort. My small god is noticeably absent now. Have I perhaps been forsaken? He's been pestering me for prayer. Maybe he thinks I'll relent in the wild?

~

I've discovered my little god is afraid of the new horizon which I uncovered this weekend. Such irony that I've been hooked up with a domestic god. A deity of home and hearth. A god more comfortable behind a walled garden or a locked door than amidst the frontiers of creation. My little god wants nothing of the larger world, and covers his ears when I speak of The Great Indifference. It's no wonder he's so jealous of others. His wrath now is no surprise. I wonder how we can reconcile our difference? Find peace between his small heaven and the greater universe of reality. I suspect I'll simply need to leave him at home when I go out. Let him alone with his certitude and finality. Deny and protect him from the vast ignorance and reality which looms like a giant before us both whenever we step foot outside our door.

~

My little god's insistence on immortality is striking given his additional claim to know everything. Shouldn't he understand his immortality cannot possibly survive my death unless I can find another to believe after I am gone?

~

My little god came to me tonight trembling, and asking after eternity. I told him I hadn't a clue, and could offer no suggestions along these lines. He went away wide-eyed and perplexed. I'll bet he's gonna make something up.

~

A benefit of not believing in ghosts is that ghosts never come to scare me. Likewise, monsters, demons, and poltergeist. They all keep their distance. The supernatural seems to only haunt the willing; the skeptical mind offering seemingly infertile soil for what is not really there.

~

My god is small because he has no ample space to live within my mind. He'd probably be a great God if I'd only believe. He resides on a dusty and neglected mental shelf where I keep my credulity and faith, a place well illuminated with doubt to keep out the vermin. He'd be much happier on a shelf with certitude *or belief, though it seems I've only enough to sustain the slightest of gods.*

~

I awoke past midnight to walk barefoot through the dark. Not far from the tent, just enough distance to unsettle whatever comfort had seeped in from the warmth of my sleeping bag, and the safety of my shelter. I so enjoy the feeling of letting go the rope to anything sound and settled. To drift for a distance naked and shivering in the cold. To stand vulnerable beneath a vast and seemingly eternal canopy of stars. That's why I reject my muse, those ghosts and my little god, less for the fact that they aren't real, and more for the desire to do without the false comfort their non-existence could never honestly provide.

FINAL THOUGHTS

Before I leave you alone

Going Alone is less about going solo into wild places, or living tolerant of solitude, or without the warm blessing of family and friends; and more about a willingness to carry on through life with a positive, optimistic spirit in spite of the perceived void-like **Indifference** of nature. It's about making life good, and just, and communal—where the responsibility for defining goodness is our own, resting on our own shoulders; with additional responsibility to live well and to also actively work to improve this good living with each passing day. You are among this tribe if you do not shy away from what you find—or do not find—in the wild, or in solitude, or in the quiet moments alone with your mind. And if you decide instead to actively do something about these discovered facts in order to make something beautiful and meaningful of your brief life and days. And if you do this of your own volition mostly—not relying on others to pave over and civilize the wild with their own unfounded explanation, excuse or dogma—then you will rise to your full stature as a person of reason, an individual of truth, someone both humbled and in awe of the uncertain night, and willing to live **The Good Life** in that dim obscure place to the end of your days, or until discovery and effort at last reveal or produce some truer light.

Continue the adventure at
goingalone.org

Be safe...
But not too safe.

EPILOGUE

"This was observable when one of those Italian boys came along with his barrel-organ, and stopped under the wide and cool shadows of the elm. With his quick professional eye he took note of the two faces watching him from the arched window, and, opening his instrument, began to scatter its melodies abroad. He had a monkey on his shoulder, dressed in a Highland plaid; and, to complete the sum of splendid attractions wherewith he presented himself to the public, there was a company of little figures, whose sphere and habitation was in the mahogany case of his organ, and whose principle of life was the music which the Italian made it his business to grind out. In all their variety of occupation,—the cobbler, the blacksmith, the soldier, the lady with her fan, the toper with his bottle, the milkmaid sitting by her cow—this fortunate little society might truly be said to enjoy a harmonious existence, and to make life literally a dance.

The Italian turned a crank; and, behold! every one of these small individuals started into the most curious vivacity. The cobbler wrought upon a shoe; the blacksmith hammered his iron, the soldier waved his glittering blade; the lady raised a tiny breeze with her fan; the jolly toper swigged lustily at his bottle; a scholar opened his book with eager thirst for knowledge, and turned his head to and fro along the page; the milkmaid energetically drained her cow; and a miser counted gold into his strong-box,—all at the same turning of a crank. Yes; and, moved by the self-same impulse, a lover saluted his mistress on her lips! Possibly some cynic, at once merry and bitter, had desired to signify, in this pantomimic scene, that we mortals, whatever our business or amusement,—however serious, however trifling,—all dance to one identical tune, and, in spite of our ridiculous activity, bring nothing finally to pass. For the most remarkable aspect of the affair was, that, at the cessation of the music, everybody was petrified at once, from the most extravagant life into a dead torpor. Neither was the cobbler's shoe finished, nor the blacksmith's iron shaped out; nor was there a drop less of brandy in the toper's bottle, nor a drop more of milk in the milkmaid's pail, nor one additional coin in the miser's strong-box, nor was the scholar a page deeper in his book. All were precisely in the same condition as before they made themselves so ridiculous by their haste to toil, to enjoy, to accumulate gold, and to become wise. Saddest of all, moreover, the lover was none the happier for the maiden's granted kiss! But, rather than swallow this last too acrid ingredient, we reject the whole moral of the show."

-Nathaniel Hawthorne

ECCLESIASTES 9

"So I reflected on all this and concluded that the righteous and the wise and what they do are in God's hands, but no one knows whether love or hate awaits them. All share a common destiny—the righteous and the wicked, the good and the bad, the clean and the unclean, those who offer sacrifices and those who do not.

As it is with the good,
so with the sinful;
as it is with those who take oaths,
so with those who are afraid to take them.

This is the evil in everything that happens under the sun: The same destiny overtakes all. The hearts of people, moreover, are full of evil and there is madness in their hearts while they live, and afterward they join the dead. Anyone who is among the living has hope—even a live dog is better off than a dead lion!

For the living know that they will die,
but the dead know nothing;
they have no further reward,
and even their name is forgotten.

Their love, their hate
and their jealousy have long since vanished;
never again will they have a part
in anything that happens under the sun.

Go, eat your food with gladness, and drink your wine with a joyful heart, for God has already approved what you do. Always be clothed in white, and always anoint your head with oil. Enjoy life with your wife, whom you love, all the days of this meaningless life that God has given you under the sun—all your meaningless days. For this is your lot in life and in your toilsome labor under the sun. Whatever your hand finds to do, do it with all your might, for in the realm of the dead, where you are going, there is neither working nor planning nor knowledge nor wisdom." [NIV]

GHOST TOWN[11]

*I recently bought two books on ghost towns. I have some
others, too. As I read in them a bit I saw the ghost towns as a
metaphor for my own life.*

*I once had some "action" going on. It may even have appeared
to others as though I was something special. People called me
and I called them. I spent time with people for both business
and personal reasons. People probably talked about me more
than I would have liked, and I am pleased that I was not
listening in. I would have been embarrassed. But now no one
does. I have become a ghost town.*

*People see me but I have no meaning in their lives at all. Some
stop by in the form of phone calls, and I do have a few
correspondents left, but that's all the visitation I receive now.
Even some of the correspondence I send does not get quickly
returned, as with Bill, June and Aunt Sally, both ladies having
finally died.*

This all reminds me of Mr. Flood's Party *by Edward Arlington
Robinson. Call me Eben Flood.*

*Ghost towns are lonely places especially at night. Where the
hotels and saloons once offered gaiety and diversion, the doors
are permanently closed now and electricity is no longer
furnished. Houses which once gave shelter and witnessed
family gatherings and I daresay procreating, well, these houses
only serve the needs of lesser creatures seeking shelter
undisturbed. The streets are completely and regrettably safe to*

313

wander. No one will bother you. The entire town now may in fact legally belong to one person, and even he or she doesn't care what happens there. The place may be worth more if it burns down. Even the wood is too old for the fireplace; the oil and resins have evaporated, the life gone out of it.

There is no chance for recovery either. Hospice is not provided for ghost towns because it is futile. I think the town feels lonely most of the time; some personal company would be most welcome. But moribund began long ago and now the fact of death is ever present, so to offer any kind of succor at all would be wasteful in a society of disruptive efficiencies.

I wonder what my name is.

"Men should be taught not to be wholly careless about their memory, but to endeavor that they may be remembered chiefly for their virtues."

-Dr. Johnson

RECOMMENDED READING

This section contains a list of my favorite books and titles worth reading as a foundation to good thought and the pursuit of your own philosophy. I've listed the books in the order in which I would read them again. There are many more books I could recommend, though sometimes some books are enough, as suggested by Seneca:

"You must linger among a limited number of master-thinkers, and digest their works, if you would derive ideas which shall win firm hold in your mind."

1. *Walden* by Henry David Thoreau
2. *Cosmos* by Carl Sagan
3. *The Scarlet Letter* by Nathaniel Hawthorn
4. *Meditations* by Marcus Aurelius (George Long translation)
5. *Moby Dick* by Herman Melville
6. *The Discourses* by Epictetus
7. *The Grapes of Wrath* by John Steinbeck
8. *Epistles* by Seneca
9. *Self Reliance* by Ralph Waldo Emerson
10. *The Selfish Gene* by Richard Dawkins
11. *The House of the Seven Gables* by Nathaniel Hawthorn
12. *Pilgrim at Tinker Creek* by Annie Dillard
13. *Code of Hammurabi*
14. *Enuma Elish* – The Babylonian Epic of Creation
15. *The Torah* with commentary by Rabbi Rashi
16. *The Bible* (King James and New International Version (NIV) editions) I read one chapter a day, beginning at the front and proceeding to the back, and then round-and-round again, every day, for all my life.
17. *On the Nature of the Universe* by Lucretius
18. *On Man in the Universe* by Aristotle

APPENDIX

1. Web address to the softypapa Facebook page where nearly all of the blurbs in this book did first appear: https://www.facebook.com/Softypapa-337676096304661

2. Web address to the "Anxiety Hike" blog post featuring photos and a map of the area: https://softypapa.wordpress.com/2017/11/15/the-anxiety-hike-going-alone
    And here is the address to the Anxiety Hike video on YouTube: https://youtu.be/Obe3mo3o34M

3. De Kehoe, Joe—The Silence and the Sun—Trails End Publishing

4. "I went to the woods because I wished to live deliberately, to front only the essential facts of life, and see if I could not learn what it had to teach, and not, when I came to die, discover that I had not lived." Author Thoreau, Henry David. Walden, chapter 2.

5. Henry David Thoreau also had a railroad, and railroad workers to reflect on during his time in the woods. He uses their example and industry in providing commentary on our curious self-domestication. From the first chapter of Walden:
    "We do not ride on the railroad; it rides upon us. Did you ever think what those sleepers are that underlie the railroad? Each one is a man, an Irishman, or a Yankee man. The rails are laid on them, and they are covered with sand, and the cars run smoothly over them. They are sound sleepers, I assure you. And every few years a new lot is laid down and run over; so that, if some have the

pleasure of riding on a rail, others have the misfortune to be ridden upon. And when they run over a man that is walking in his sleep, a supernumerary sleeper in the wrong position, and wake him up, they suddenly stop the cars, and make a hue and cry about it, as if this were an exception. I am glad to know that it takes a gang of men for every five miles to keep the sleepers down and level in their beds as it is, for this is a sign that they may sometime get up again."

6. There's a surprise waiting in one of those dykes. It's been waiting there since 1932. Searching the web for a miner named "Louis W. Osborne" will give you a clue. When you arrive, look at the rocks. Look CLOSELY at the rocks.

7. The entries within this section did originally include photographic illustrations. These can be seen at the following URL: https://softypapa.wordpress.com/writing/journal/the-path-of-wildness-2/the-path-of-wildness-memes

8. This passage is reminiscent of lines from Walden where Henry David Thoreau describes his neighbors moving along the highway of life with their various and excess goods, merchandise and possessions weighing them down from more worthy pursuits:
    "How many a poor immortal soul have I met well-nigh crushed and smothered under its load, creeping down the road of life, pushing before it a barn seventy-five feet by forty, its Augean stables never cleansed, and one hundred acres of land, tillage, mowing, pasture, and wood-lot. The portionless, who struggle with no such unnecessary inherited encumbrances, find it labor enough to subdue

and cultivate a few cubic feet of flesh."

9. Web address to the YouTube playlist "The Good Life" https://www.youtube.com/playlist?list=PLsxz6VpLrYyPhB kcJc8qu_QCZZz2C1Url

10. This passage is my homage to Diogenes of Sinope, the Greek cynic who lived in a barrel, preferred the company of dogs and who made a virtue of poverty.

11. This short essay "Ghost Town" was given to me by a very learned and wise man in the last season of his life, writing about his experience, place, and circumstance. It is a cautionary tale, perhaps directed at the young who may yet be fooling themselves that there is ever time to come, and that relevance persists, and that someone will certainly be there to hear our tale when at last we are ready to speak. Speak now. For ghost towns are truly real.

Printed in Great Britain
by Amazon

45672015R00182